KU-151-018

Irish Lighthouses

Sharma Krauskopf

WITHDRAWN
FROM
STOCK

Appletree Press

187088|

387·155

First published in 2001 by
Appletree Press Ltd
The Old Potato Station
14 Howard Street South
Belfast BT7 1AP
Tel: (0) 28 90 243074
Fax: (0) 28 90 246756
E-mail: reception@appletree.ie
Web Site: www.appletree.ie

Copyright © Appletree Press Ltd, 2001.

Printed in Singapore. All rights reserved. No part of this publication may be reproduced or transmitted in any
form or by any means, electronic or mechanical, photocopying, recording or in any information and retrieval
system without prior permission in writing from the publisher.

A catalogue record for this book is available from the British Library.

Irish Lighthouses

ISBN 0-86281-804-4

10 9 8 7 6 5 4 3 2 1

The publisher wishes to thank the following for permission to publish photographs on the pages listed:
Liam Blake at Imagefile pp 7 (bottom), 12, 13 (top & bottom), 14, 17, 18, 25 (top), 26, 31, 48, 56, 68, 82, 95;
Imagefile p 30; Imagefile (Richard Cummins) pp 6, 7 (top), 11, 19, 23, 24, 25 (bottom), 27, 28, 37, 38, 43, 64,
73, 76; Imagefile (Jamie Blandford) pp 9, 10; Imagefile (John Murray) p47; Imagefile (Christopher Ramsay) pp
60, 61; Imagefile (George Munday) p 53; Imagefile (Peter Zoeller) pp 66–7; John Eagle pp 8, 16, 20, 21, 33 (top
and bottom), 34, 35, 39, 40, 41, 42, 44, 45, 50, 51, 52, 54, 57, 58, 63, 88; The Irish Stock Library pp 74–5, 77,
78; Philip Plisson/Pêcheur D'Images pp 49, 62, 69, 71. Map: © Maps in Minutes™ 2001. ©Crown Copyright,
Ordnance Survey Northern Ireland 2001 Permit No. NI 1675 & ©Government of Ireland, Ordnance Survey
Ireland.

Editor: Paul Harron
Designer: Wayne Matier
Copy-editing by Robert Blackwell

Books by Sharma Krauskopf:

Scotland – The Complete Guide
Scottish Lighthouses
The Last Lighthouse

For children:
Moonbeam Cow

This book is dedicated to my brother, Raymond Morrison, and his wife Marylou, who loved Ireland so much on our latest trip.

Contents

INTRODUCTION

Living in the lighthouse keeper's accommodation at Eshaness in the Shetland Islands, I have for long had a fascination with lighthouses. Having visited Ireland many times, it seemed only natural to combine my love of Ireland with my affinity for lighthouses.

With almost 1,980 miles (3,168 km) of coastline, lighthouses have played an important role in the history of Ireland. The country's first lighthouse was built at Hook Head in the fifth century when St Dubhán, who came from Wales, built his living quarters and a beacon light on the south end of Hy-Kinsellagh. This makes him Ireland's first lighthouse keeper. Many feel he should be recognised as the patron saint of the Irish lighthouse service for his endeavours. This first light was a tower surrounding an iron basket in which he burned whatever he could find such as coal, wood or tar. There has been a lighthouse in that area ever since, although it has not always been operational.

The Baily

The next oldest lighthouse is Youghal. It was established in 1190 by Maurice Fitzgerald and was in the custody of the nuns of St Anne's Convent until 1542. M. Boullaye le Gouz referred to it in his tour of the country in 1644 as "formerly part of a convent of nuns of which there remains a tower called the Nunnery, upon which they used to light torches to enable vessels to come into the harbour during the night".

In the early 1700s, the building of lighthouses began with a simple cottage and an open coal fire in a chauffer on the roof at Charlesport in 1665. This was followed by Baily lighthouse and another on the Kinsale Peninsula called Old Head. From these humble beginnings, there are now over 80 lighthouses in operation.

The Commissioners of Irish Lights (CIL), who are responsible for operating the Irish lighthouse system, maintain 82 unmanned lighthouses, 1 fog signal station, 2 light vessels, 2 large automated navigational buoys, 2 lighted and 17 unlighted beacons, 2 lighted and 27 unlighted perches, 130 solar-powered buoys, 1 electric-powered buoy, 15 unlighted buoys and 1 mooring. They also operate 7 helicopter bases, 21 radar beacons and 3 Marine DGPS beacons. The CIL are the general lighthouse authority for the entire island of Ireland, its adjacent seas and islands. They are dedicated to providing the latest aids to navigation service for all mariners at the least possible cost and in compliance with national and international obligations. Their motto is "*In salutem omnium*", which means "For the safety of all". Further duties for the CIL regard wreck marking and removal, and the inspection and approval of aids to navigation provided by ports and local lighthouse authorities in Ireland. The CIL was founded in 1867, although its origins can be traced back to 1665 when Charles II granted permission to Sir Richard Reading to erect six lighthouses on the Irish coast.

A significant piece of lighthouse history was created when the Republic of Ireland was created. In 1938, an agreement that repealed the right of the British Government to re-occupy the southern Irish ports also repealed their right to take over the Irish lights. It was decided to keep just one body to control all of the lighthouses of Ireland. However, Northern Ireland was given adequate representation on the CIL.

A frequent question when looking at lighthouse history is how they are funded. When a ship docks at any port in the UK or Ireland, she is charged light dues at a rate dependent on her weight. Although pleasure craft weighing less than 20 tons and fishing vessels registered in Ireland are major beneficiaries, they are exempt from these charges. The funds raised are put into a General Lighthouse Fund (GLF) administered by the Department of Environment, Transport and the Regions (DETR). The biggest contributor to the GLF is foreign shipping. The money is allocated to the various lighthouse authorities according to their needs through a process of assessment that includes shipowners and all the lighthouse authorities involved. The Irish Government's Department of Marine and Natural Resources also makes a grant in aid to the GLF.

Old Head of Kinsale

As in most countries, Irish lights could be historically categorised into three types. First, and the ones that most people get to see, were the land stations. Land stations were manned with the keepers' families living in accommodation near or attached to the light. Baily and Hook Head are examples of this type of light. The second category was relieving stations with dwellings ashore for the keepers' families. The dwellings were often located in the closest mainland area. An example of this type of arrangement is the

Hook Head

N

S

Eagle Island

Maidens where the keepers' accommodation is in Larne. The final category is the relieving and non-dwelling stations on remote rock lights. Blackrock Mayo, Fastnet and Eagle Island are all examples of this type.

At one time, there was another category of lights called "unwatched" that never had keepers, such as miniature lighthouses or pile lights. The term "unwatched" technically meant that no one "watches" the lights on a four-hour on and eight-hours off schedule. Today, all the Irish lighthouses are "unwatched" since all of the keepers are now gone. They are all automated with a local attendant checking the facility on a periodic basis.

This book features 36 lighthouses from all over Ireland. It gives examples of all the different kinds of lights built there. I selected lights on a very subjective basis; I was either fascinated by the lighthouse for some aesthetic or historical reason. There are 46 more lighthouses in Ireland that I could have included. However, by including those that I consider to be the most striking, I hope it will go some way in encouraging the reader to go and visit the remaining lights. We begin looking at lighthouses on the eastern coast of the Republic of Ireland and travel clockwise around the island eventually ending up with Northern Ireland's lights .

One difficulty that faces anyone compiling a guide to Ireland is the variant spelling of place names. For consistency, I have used the spelling on a recently printed map (Collins All Ireland Road Map [9 miles to 1 inch], HarperCollins, 2000).

a boat or helicopter. Ferries, running from Rosslare to Fishguard and Pembroke, do, however, give a good view of the lighthouse.

Next to the ferry terminal is the CIL Depot. You can sometimes see buoys in the yard waiting for overhaul or a light vessel in the harbour pending repairs or relocation. Often the ships are marked on their side with the name of the station they are heading to or from.

Hook Head

Dating from the fifth century, Hook Head (navigational location 52° 7.3' N 6° 55.7' W) is thought to be one of the four oldest lighthouses in the world. It is the oldest lighthouse in the British Isles. Dubhán, a Welsh monk, was thought to have established the first light. "Rinn Dubhain" was the name he gave to this remote part of the County Wexford coast. The Irish translation of Dubhán is "fishing hook", which led to the current name Point of the Hook.

Dubhán chose this place for its remoteness, being surrounded on three sides by the sea. He built a cell and oratory on the southern end of the point at Churchtown, where the ruined church of St Saviour can be found. Soon after the establishment of his cell, he began to find mariners and wreckage on the beach below. He saved as many of the shipwrecked as he could and the dead he buried. Dubhán decided to make an effort to warn the ships away from Rinn Dubhain. With the help of a local blacksmith, he built a chauffer, which was a huge iron basket that hung over the cliff. At sunset, he would build a fire in the chauffer and keep it burning during the night. He used what he had for fuel such as coal, wood and charcoal; the most plentiful fuel was the driftwood collected from the ships wrecked on the peninsula.

Upon the death of Dubhán, fellow monks who had joined his community tended the light. They kept the watch until approximately 50 years before the Anglo-Norman invasion. Since monks tended the light, it was called an ecclesiastical light. It is believed that the

Hook Head

*Hook Head
at dawn*

monks encouraged donations to the light by granting indulgences to the donors.

Around 1172, the Tower of Hook, an 80-foot (25 m) high fortress and watchtower, was built by the newly arrived Normans in a strategic location at the end of the two-mile (3 km) long peninsula. Folklore maintains that either Eva, Strongbow's wife, or Raymond le Gros, husband of Strongbow's only sister, Basilia, built it and the monks were given the responsilbity of taking care of it. The Bailiffs of New Ross were given custody of the tower in 1307 but the monks continued to maintain it. Laypersons took over the care of the light when the monks left before the dissolution of the monasteries in Ireland in the sixteenth century.

After more than 800 years, the tower is still in exceptional condition. Walls measuring between 9 and 13 feet (3-4 m) with stone steps leading to the top of the tower can still be seen. Each of the tower's three levels has a vaulted construction with windows in embrasures. Fuel was stored in the first story. The Assistant Keeper lived on the second floor and the Principal Keeper on the third.

In the early seventeenth century, the lighthouse became a centre for counterfeiting money. It was a great location for any illegal activity as it was removed from civilisation and any visitors could be seen before they arrived.

In the late 1600s, the lighthouse was uninhabited and no light shown. In 1657, the Commissioners of Public Revenue were petitioned by merchants, shipowners and mariners to restore the lighthouse on Hook Head. Nothing happened until 1665, when King Charles II granted a franchise to Sir Robert Reading to build six lighthouses, one of which was on Hook Head. Around 1677, Hook Head was re-lit. A special lantern was built to act as the beacon. It had a fire-proof brick dome with a flue to conduct the smoke away from the flame. During Sir Robert Reading's supervision, the height of the tower was increased by approximately 20 feet (6 m) and the width by 12 feet (4 m). The current tower is 115 feet (35 m) tall.

Near the end of the eighteenth century, the tower fell into disrepair and ex-Trinity House engineer Thomas Rogers was given the responsibility of maintaining and staffing Hook Head by the Revenue Commissioners. He installed a new 12-feet (4 m) diameter lantern and 12 Argand oil lamps with reflectors. Two years later, the lantern was again improved and in 1864 a fixed dioptric lens replaced the old lantern. Currently, the lantern flashes white every 3 seconds and has a nominal range of 23 nautical miles. Its day mark is a white tower with two black bands.

A fog-warning device was first added in the form of a bell but it proved to be inadequate. In 1872, the bell was replaced by a gun, which was then replaced by an explosive charge in 1905. Keeping the explosives secure was a problem, so a Supertyfon Emitter operated by compressed air was used in place of the explosive-charged horn. Racon for increased safety was added to the station in 1974.

The keepers were withdrawn in 1977. The facilities are now being turned into a heritage visitor centre. In the monastery, the second floor of the lighthouse, visitors can hear an audio show about the lighthouse and the legend of Dubhán. The first floor chambers where the light keepers lived are on display. There is a 115-step climb to the parapet with panoramic views of the area. There is also a café and craft shop in the former keepers' houses.

Another claim to fame for this area is the origin of the well-known phrase "by hook or by crook". In 1170, Robert FitzGilbert de Clare, Earl Of Pembroke, better known as Strongbow, landed here on his way to capture Waterford. He instructed his men to land "by Hook or by Crooke" as the settlement at Crooke was another accessible landing point across the harbour from Hook.

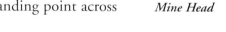

Mine Head

If you would like to visit the facility, it can be found on the east side of Waterford Harbour. From New Ross, take the R739 south towards Arthurstown and follow the coast of the harbour to the peninsula's end at Churchtown.

Mine Head

George Halpin Senior designed the major light of Mine Head, located a few miles south of Helving Head at the south end of Dungarvan Bay (navigational location 51°

*Mine Head
at sunset*

59.6' N 7° 35.2' W). The red sandstone structure sitting on top of the steep cliffs between Dungarvan and Ardmore is higher above the water than any other Irish lighthouse. It is 285 feet (88 m) above sea-level.

Local merchants and mariners from Youghal and Cork pressured the Ballast Board to begin a lighthouse tower on Capel Island off Youghal. This building was begun even though George Halpin felt the best place for a light was on Mine Head. The work was well under-way when the local people changed their mind and decided that the light should be at Mine Head after all. After much debate, including input from Trinity House and the Admiralty, it was decided to abandon the site on Capel Island and build on Mine Head. The light was established on 1 June 1851, the same day as Ballycotton.

Mine Head has a 70-foot (22 m) white tower with a black band. It was converted to electricity in September 1964. The beacon flashes white and red every 2.5 seconds and has a nominal range of 28 nautical miles since it sits so high above sea-level. The keepers were removed on 20 August 1973.

An example of the earliest megalithic tombs in Ireland, commonly known as court tombs, is to be found in the area of the lighthouse. The name comes from the fact that this type of tomb usually has a courtyard area found at the entrance to the chambers. A court cairn is situated in Ballinamona Lower, Parish of Ardmore. The site is marked "dolmen" on the Ordnance Survey map, and is known locally as "Cailleach Bhearra's House". It is located about one mile (1.6 km) north of Mine Head lighthouse and about 100 yards (92 m) from the cliff edge.

To find the lighthouse and cairn head south from Dungarvan on the N25. After ten miles (16 km), you will come to the junction of the N25 and D53. Turn left and continue until you come to a crossroads. Turn right at the post office and head downhill towards the sea. The second road to the left is a narrow lane leading to two houses and the lighthouse. The road is signposted "Slow" and "Do not approach". A bungalow is just beyond the signs and you should ask permission here to go any further since it is a private road. When you reach the lighthouse and the cairn, be careful as the cliffs can be dangerous, particularly in the spring when they have been weakened by winter storms.

Ballycotton

The grounding of the steamship *Sirius* on Smith's Rock west of Ballycotton in 1847 strengthened the argument for putting more lighthouses around Cork Harbour. The *Sirius* was famous because in 1838 she was the first steamship to travel westward across the Atlantic Ocean using only steam power. The problem was where to build the lighthouse. A group including the Cork Steamship Company wanted the Ballast Board to complete the structure begun on Capel Island, but the Cork Harbour Board preferred a new light to be built on Ballycotton Island. The Ballast Board asked for an opinion from the Admiralty, which gave a usual bureaucratic answer: "determine a course that seems best calculated for the benefit of the public".

Ballycotton

Leabharlann 181088 Contae na Mí

The Ballast Board directed that all construction be stopped on Capel Island lighthouse and recommended dismantling the 6-foot (2 m) tower on Capel and moving it to Ballycotton. This was not feasible, so it was finally decided that a new light would be built at Ballycotton and at Mine Head.

Ballycotton Island, just off the southern tip of Ballycotton Bay, was purchased from the Archbishop of Dublin and the Bishop of Cork for one shilling each. George Halpin Senior designed the tower and the keepers' accommodation on Ballycotton Island (navigational location 51° 49.5' N 7° 59.1' W). Red sandstone quarried on the island was used to build the facility. The light was established on 1 June 1851, the same day as Mine Head.

The lantern was a catadioptric apparatus with a fixed inner optic and a rotating outer, the first of this type to be used in Ireland. The beacon had eight faces, each with an angular lens and a set of condensing prisms. The light sources were multiple wick oil lamps, which radiated a beam through each of the eight lenses. The character of the light at that time was flashing white every 10 seconds. The lighthouse could be seen 18 miles (29 km) out to sea on a good day. Currently, the character of the light is flashing white and red every 10 seconds with a nominal range of 21 nautical miles in white and 17 in red.

When the fifty-foot (15 m) tower was built 195 feet (60 m) above the sea, it was the colour of the natural stone whilst the accommodation was painted white. In order to give it a more distinctive day mark, the tower was painted in 1892 with a black band in the middle of the tower, and finally, in 1902, the tower was painted its current black.

The area around Ballycotton has frequent and dense fog so a foghorn was added to the station in 1856. A beautiful belfry was built to hold a bell, which functioned until 1908. The bell was replaced in 1909 with a reed horn, which blew 6 times every 2 minutes. In 1924, the reed horn was replaced with an "A" type diaphone with the same character. Today, the foghorn blows 4 times every 90 seconds. The light is exhibited by day when the fog signal is sounding.

In 1975, the original optic was replaced with an AGA sealed-beam lamp array, the facility converted to electricity and a helipad added. The keepers' families had been moved ashore in 1896 but new quarters were built for the keepers and visitors with a watchtower on the roof.

Ballycotton lighthouse was a favourite among the keepers and became known as the "Ballycotton Hilton". The keepers performed many rescues such as saving four Dutch fishermen whose boat went aground on the rocks near the lighthouse. The keepers were able to reach the sailors and carry them up the steep slope to safety. The lighthouse was automated in 1992 and the keepers removed.

The light vessel *Daunt* went adrift for three days off the Cork coast near Ballycotton lighthouse in 1936 in a fierce southeasterly gale. Rescue was attempted by the Ballycotton lifeboat, the *SS Innisfallen* out of Cork, the *HMS Tenedos* and *SS Isolda*. The rescue was successful with no casualties. A stamp was issued commemorating the event in 1974.

If you would like to see this lighthouse, go to Ballycotton by taking the N25 west from Youghal and turning south at Castlemartyr on the R632 watching for signs. The lighthouse is offshore on an island. The best way to see it is to ask a local boat owner to take you for a trip around the island. The Cliffstop Café in Ballycotton at the top of the hill has the best views of the lighthouse.

Roche's Point

An existing 35-foot (11 m) watchtower, Roche's Tower on Roche's Point, was suggested as an ideal location to build a lighthouse to light the mouth of Cork Harbour in the early nineteenth century. The tower stood 46 feet (14 m) above the water and was high enough for a lighthouse. It was built by either Edward Roche Esquire of Trabolgan or his father and was often described by town folk as "a banqueting and pleasure house, built by the Roche family to afford them a good view of Cork Harbour and the movement of shipping". It had been rented during the last half of the eighteenth century to the Government as a watchtower. It took two years to negotiate the sale with the Roche family as the owner was in Italy. He was thought to be a soldier of fortune who had ended up in an Italian jail as a prisoner of war.

The negotiations took so long that George Halpin Senior designed a new lighthouse with a granite tower for the site. The tower was squat, being only 36 feet (11 m) tall and 6 feet (2 m) in diameter. However, the headland it was built on was high so the lantern stood 92 feet (28 m) above the sea. The light was established on 4 June 1817 (navigational location 51° 47.6' N 8° 15.3' W).

As Cork Harbour shipping grew, it was felt that the tower was too small. In 1835, the tower was dismantled and replaced by the present tower, which stands 49 feet (15 m) high and 12 feet (3.7 m) wide. The lantern, lighting apparatus and all of the bricks from the old tower were shipped to Duncannon in County Wexford and rebuilt into Duncannon North light in 1838.

Roche's Point

Currently, the character of Roche's Point is flashing white and red every 3 seconds. A second-order Fresnel lens is still in use. The white beam has a nominal range of 20 nautical miles and the red 16 miles. The tower is currently painted white for a day mark with an orange railing around the tower.

On 1 April 1995, Roche's Point was automated and the following statement released by the CIL: "At Roche's Point, the lighthouse compound has been contracted into a smaller area encompassing the tower, adjacent dwelling and engine house. With the exception of the old buoy bank store all the other dwellings and buildings on the site have been sold at public auction. The redundant manual buoy crane at the landing has been dismantled and removed. The old familiar pneumatic fog signal at Roche's Point could not be converted for automatic operation and it has been removed and replaced by a new electric fog signal with a range of 4 nautical miles. This change has not been universally welcomed by local residents; however, in time it will no doubt be accepted".

The area is a great place to visit. From the lighthouse, you can look across the entrance of Cork Harbour, with its splendid and varied traffic of yachts, trawlers, cargo ships and assorted small boats.

The Royal Cork Yacht Club is the oldest yacht club in the world. It was founded in 1720 and is only a few minutes from the lighthouse. Its first clubhouse was situated in a castle on Haulbowline Island in Cork Harbour, which now forms part of the naval base. Sometime shortly before 1806, the club moved to the town of Cove. In 1966, the Royal Cork and the Royal Munster Yacht clubs agreed to merge and the Royal Cork moved to its present premises in Crosshaven.

The lighthouse is situated about 15 minutes from Midleton near the main road to Rosslare. When you reach Midleton, turn and follow the signs to Whitegate. Keep on the main road out of Whitegate, passing a large industrial complex on a hill. Just beyond the industrial complex, turn right and follow the road to the end where you will be able to see the lighthouse.

*Old Head
of Kinsale*

Old Head of Kinsale

The steep rocky cliff on the peninsula of Old Head, or Capo de Vel (Cape of Light) as the Spaniards called it, has had many lighthouses (navigational location 51° 36.3' N 8° 31.9' W). It is believed that Celtic settlers built the first beacon on the Cape of Light as early as 100 BC to mislead ships into rocks so they could be plundered.

The harbour is landlocked and has always been busy with fishing, trading and shipbuilding since there was lumber available on Compass Hill. Fishing declined at times as a result of foreign boats fishing too far inland and the Penal Laws on fishermen, only to return to new heights. The increased fishing brought steam-powered ships from all over England and Europe to purchase the catch. With increased marine traffic, a light was needed on Old Head as it was then called.

Sir Robert Reading was given the franchise in 1665 to build a simple cottage-type lighthouse. The small house in which the keeper lived had an open coal fire in a chauffer on its roof. Sir Robert Reading charged high tolls and operating fees to mariners using the port instead of passing ships offshore. English shipowners complained that the fees were too high and so the British Parliament made English and Irish shipping exempt from the tolls. In compensation, they gave Reading £500 a year to operate the lighthouse. For 15 years it functioned well, but in 1681 the light was put out and the house abandoned and allowed deteriorate for the next 20 years.

A petition sent to the House of Commons on 18 November 1703 from the sovereign burgesses and commonalty of Kinsale asked that the light be re-lit since it had been "unreasonably discontinued for upward of 20 years". The State took over the running of the light for more than 50 years.

As the fishing industry continued to boom in the nineteenth century, the Revenue Commissioners, the Irish lighthouse authority in 1804, decided to replace the old fire-burning beacon with a temporary lantern. Thomas Rogers, the Commissioner's lighting contractor, built a temporary 6-foot (2 m) diameter lantern with 12

*Old Head light
at night*

Old Head from the sea

oil lamps and reflectors. This lantern operated for the next eight years. It is rumoured that the keepers' accommodation was used for all kinds of illicit activities during this time, including prostitution and counterfeiting.

The Revenue Commissioners gave up control of the Irish lights to the Ballast Board in the early 1800s. One of the Ballast Board's first instructions was to have Inspector George Halpin Senior inspect Old Head. He recommended, due to the run-down condition of the facility and the heavy traffic in the port of Kinsale, that a new permanent tower with a modern lens should replace the lighthouse. The Board agreed and George Halpin designed a facility that was built for a little under £10,000. A fixed white light was established on 16 May 1814 with a range of 23 nautical miles. The tower stood 294 feet (90 m) above the water and had a lantern with 27 Argand oil lamps each with its own parabolic reflector. The tower and houses were painted white for a day marker.

In July 1843, the Elder Brethren of Trinity visited the headland and in their report strongly criticised the Old Head light as being too high and often obscured by fog and low clouds. George Halpin agreed with them. In 1846, a new lighthouse was built on the promontory point. The new light had a tower of 98 foot (30 m) that stood 236 feet (73 m) above the water. The tower was painted white with two red bands and the light established in 1853. Not only was the old 1814-tower discontinued it was shortened so that ships would not get confused. The stones removed from the tower were used to build Horse Rock beacon. A foghorn of 3 cannons, which fired 2 times every 10 minutes, was installed in 1893.

The Mercantile Marine Service Association became concerned about the quality of the light at Old Head and asked the CIL to strengthen the light. Two years later, a proposal went to Trinity House for their approval. An iron lantern with a double flashing, incandescent, vaporised paraffin iron lantern replaced the old lantern. The foghorn was replaced with 2 successive blasts every 6 minutes from a cotton-powder charge. This new arrangement was established on 17 December 1907. It was changed again in 1972 when the explosive foghorn was replaced with a siren that came from the Power Head Fog Signal Station. Also in 1973, the lantern was changed to electricity with a standby generator. The current character of the light is 2 white flashes every 10 seconds and the foghorn 3 signals every 45 seconds. Today's day mark is a black tower with two white bands.

The light was unwatched and automated on 1 April 1987. Currently, an attendant lives on the premises to maintain the light.

The area will always be well known for the sinking of the luxury liner *Lusitania* on 7 May1915. A U-20 submarine lay in wait 26 miles (42 km) from Queenstown. The *Lusitania* was torpedoed twice without warning at 2.15 pm, 8 miles (13 km) from the Head of Kinsale in sight of the lighthouse. The ship sank in less than one hour. SOS messages were sent, lifeboats lowered and fishing and other craft were quickly on the scene before larger boats from Queenstown arrived. Records show 746 passengers rescued while 1,142 were drowned. Unknown to most at that time, 1,198 people had remained on the ship, including 785 passengers. Of those left on the ship, 94 were children and 35 of them were under 4-years-old. Among those drowned were 124 prominent Americans. This provoked resentment in America and ten days later President Wilson sent his first note to Berlin where he stated that neutral shipping should be left in peace. The Germans claimed *Lusitania* was armed and warned but the US disputed this assertion.

If you would like to visit the lighthouse, take the R600 from Kinsale until you come to Ballinspittle where you turn south. Drive until you come to the sign for Old Head. Follow this road until you can see the lighthouse.

Galley Head

Five miles (8 km) southeast of Rosscarbery in County Cork can be found Galley Head lighthouse sitting on Dundeady Island (navigational location 51° 31.7' N 8° 57.1' W). Dundeady is not an island but joined to the mainland by a strip of land. It took years of perseverance from a local nobleman, Lord Bandon, imploring those in power to get permission for a lighthouse to be built there.

Galley Head

Galley Head light

The responsibility for building the new light was given to J.S. Sloan, Engineer-in-Chief to the CIL. It was established on 1 January 1878. Gas made from cannel coal was chosen as the source. The contractors, Messrs Edmundson & Co of Dublin, built the lantern, a French-made optic, as well as a specially designed gas works on the station's grounds. The beacon consisted of four tiers of overlaid optics. The number of layers ignited would depend on the weather. The keeper began with only one optic being lighted but as the weather worsened additional layers would be lit. The gas-powered light had a range of 19 miles (30 km) from the 69-foot (21 m) tower that sat at the edge of the steep cliff.

Local legend tells how the Sultan of Turkey, a guest of Lord Carbery at Castle Free, asked why the lighthouse did not shine on land. Lord Carbery, embarrassed by the Sultan's question, talked to the CIL and had six panes on the dark landward side replaced with clear glass so that the light would shine on the land also. When the tower was converted to electricity, the clear panes were painted black so that the light would not blind passing motorists.

With an increase of candlepower in the optic in 1907, the nominal range rose to 24 nautical miles. When the conversion to electricity was made in 1969, the candlepower was again increased from 262,000 to 2.8 million and the range to 28 nautical miles. The current nominal range is 23 nautical miles with a character of 5 white flashes every 20 seconds. The station at Galley Head is an extremely efficient and well-built facility. The facility is totally surrounded by a white wall. A 125-foot (38 m) passageway leads to the two-story building that contained the gas works. The station was automated and the keepers removed on 31 January 1997.

Because of the number of shipwrecks in the area of Galley Head, diving is an increasingly popular sport. The area was an important theatre in developing submarine warfare during the Great War. One of the most famous of the shipwrecks off Galley Head is known as "The Silver Dollar Wreck". The steamer and sailor *The Crescent City* ran aground against the Doolic Rock and sank on 2 February 1871. Part of the ship's cargo was 40 boxes containing 240,000 Mexican silver dollars valued at £110,000. Today, she lies upright in 115 feet (35 m) of water only a few hundred feet from the lighthouse. Legend says that the silver dollars are still in her hold.

Other wrecks for diving include the Honk Kong-registered ore/bulk/oil motor vessel *Kowloon Bridge*. She became a total loss when she was wrecked off the southern coast of Ireland. The *Kowloon Bridge* was on a voyage from St Lawrence River Port of Seven Islands, Quebec, on 7 February 1886 bound for the River Clyde terminal of Hunterston, loaded with a cargo of 160,000 tons of iron ore consigned to the British Steel Corporation. However, en route she had to seek shelter in Bantry Bay to effect repairs to deck cracks sustained during heavy Atlantic weather. On 22 November, she sailed out of Bantry Bay but then lost her steerage and began to drift in continuing heavy seas. The 28-man crew decided to abandon ship and were winched to safety by helicopters in enormous seas. The helpless vessel was then driven aground in gale-force winds on Stag Rock, near Baltimore, County Cork. Her 1,200 tons of bunker fuel began to leak causing a serious pollution problem to nearby coves and beaches. The *Kowloon Bridge* is believed to be the largest shipwreck in Europe and is spectacular both as a wreck and as a reef thriving with fish life. An intact U-boat (U-260) south of Glandore draws enthusiasts to view the Zeiss optics, periscopes and aerials as she lies in the eerie depths. Divers will also find offshore pinnacles festooned with jewel anemones and corals washed by clean Atlantic waters.

Shipwrecks are not all the area offers. In 1860, The *Irish Times* reported that Samuel Townsend saw a 25-30 foot (8-9 m) sea serpent surface in Whitehall Harbour. It was said that the neck of the creature was 6 feet (2 m) long. In 1953, Ray Bradbury, while living in Dublin, wrote his wonderful short story *The Fog Horn* about a dinosaur that comes from the sea and falls in love with a lighthouse foghorn.

You can reach the lighthouse by driving south from Cork on the M71 until you come to Rosscarbery. Turn left on the R598, which will take you along the coast and you can see the lighthouse off in the distance. Follow the road until you come to a dead end sign, turn right and follow that road to its end and the lighthouse will be straight ahead of you.

Fastnet

The Fastnet lighthouse sits on a clay slate (containing some quartz) pinnacle of rock about 328 feet (101 m) long and 164 feet (50 m) across. It lies a little over 4 miles (6 km) off the coast of West Cork in Roaringwater Bay.

There are many folk-tales about the rock. One tells how a giant picked up the rock, which is now the Fastnet, from Mount Gabriel near Ballydehob and hurled it into the sea. Another story says that since the rock looks like a ship under sail from a distance it sails annually to visit Bull, Calf, Cow and Heifer Rocks. There are actually two rocks in the area: Fastnet Rock, which stands 98 feet (30 m) above low water and south of it Little Fastnet, which is separated from the main rock by a 30-foot (9 m) wide channel.

Its Gaelic name, "Carrig Aonar" (lonely rock), is significant, for a lonelier place than Fastnet would be difficult to imagine. Surrounded by white water to a depth of 12 feet (4 m) with a tidal current that runs at 3 knots at times, it is possible for men to land on the rock by boat only 10 or 12 times a year. In winter, the seas reach the top of the 155-foot lighthouse tower. Fog is extremely bad in this area with zero visibility occurring many times a year. It earned itself the name "teardrop of Ireland" or "the eye of Europe" because it was the last bit of Ireland seen by thousands of immigrants on their journey to America. Its nearest neighbour to the south is the South Pole.

Fastnet lighthouse was built as a result of a terrible accident. On 15 November 1847, *The Stephen Whitney* with 110 passengers and crew aboard was wrecked on West Calf Island in the channel between the village of Schull and Cape Clear Island. The Captain and Second Mate, along with 90 others, were lost in the disaster. *The Sirius* and *Lady Flora Hasting* met adversity in nearby waters. In the years preceding this shipwreck, pleas had been made after each wreck for a serious evaluation of the locations of the lighthouses on the southern Cork coast. Cape Clear lighthouse, 450 feet (138 m) above sea-level, was too high and most of the time invisible because of fog. *The Stephen Whitney* misread the light on Rock Island for that of Old Head on Kinsale because Cape Clear was fogged in. A local newspaper reporter for the *Cork Examiner* interviewed survivors and wrote, "The ship was doomed. A brief moment only ensued, and one terrific crash followed, which instantly consigned numbers of souls to eternity. This single encounter stove in the entire side of the vessel, and in less than half an hour there were not two planks together, nor a single article of any description that could afford the means of escape to either passenger or sailor".

Fastnet

Trinity House supported the Dublin Ballast Board's proposal for the building of a lighthouse on Fastnet Rock with this statement: "The old light on Cape Clear should be extinguished, on the representation that it is too far inside the outlying dangers, such as Fastnet Rock, and at so high an elevation that it is frequently obscured by fog".

George Halpin, Senior Engineer to the Port of Dublin Corporation, was chosen to design the Fastnet tower. He built a 91-foot (28 m) tower made of cast-iron flanged plates varying in thickness from 1 3/8 inches (35 mm) at the bottom to 7/8 inches (22 mm) at the top. The top held a 28-foot (9 m) lantern. The bottom flanges were fastened to the rock with 2-foot (0.6 m) bolts. The base was 4-foot (1.2 m) thick masonry. Construction began in 1849 and the light was established on 1 January in 1854 at a cost of £17,900 (navigational location 51° 23.3' N 9° 36.1' W). Halpin died soon after the completion of the project. The light source was oil burning with a radiance of 38,000 candlepower, which flashed for 15 seconds every 2 minutes. The oil was stored in the tower and the keepers lived in barracks on the northeast side of the rocks. The extreme difficulty of landing boats on the rock led to the keepers' families being placed on the mainland at Rock Island near Crookhaven.

For ten years, Halpin's lighthouse, as this light was called, functioned as originally built. In strong gales and heavy seas, the tower would shake. Even pieces of the rock on which the tower was built were torn off by the sea and thrown at the tower. After many inspections and much discussion, the tower was strengthened. Nothing could be done to secure the keepers' accommodation so they were moved into the upper part of the tower. These adjustments seemed to work as for the next 14 years Halpin's lighthouse stood strong against the fury of the sea.

In 1867, the Dublin Port Act was passed changing the Corporation of the Port of Dublin and establishing the Commissioners of Irish Lights to take care of the lighthouses. The new Commissioners changed Fastnet's light character to one flash every minute along with other changes. On 26 November 1881, a gigantic storm hit the lighthouse and the Fastnet lantern was shattered with one lens being destroyed. The keepers were in the lower part of the tower at the time and no one was hurt. These events prompted the new Commissioners to consider alternative measures for Fastnet. Ten years later in November 1891, the Commissioners decided that the tower must be improved. William Douglass, Engineer-in-Chief of Irish Lights, was given the task of designing the new building.

Construction of a granite tower at Fastnet began in 1895. Its construction was slow and frustrating. There are 2,074 Dublin granite blocks in the tower, weighting 4,300 tons arranged in 89 courses. It is believed that the structure would not have been built without the strong leadership of James Kavanagh, the project's foreman. He led the difficult task for seven years until he became ill and died in July 1903. It was a shame that he did not see the project completed but at least the tower was done before he died as the last stone was set on 2 May 1903.

A temporary light was exhibited on 19 May 1903 on the new tower, which was to be replaced by a new light designed by C.W. Scott. The latter was finally exhibited on 27 June 1904. The new light worked beautifully as was documented in a report by Sir Robert Ball, the Commissioners' Scientific Adviser: "As to the beams of the Fastnet during all the time of our return to harbour, I cannot describe them otherwise than by saying they were magnificent... It is a matter of congratulations to everyone concerned that Fastnet is now, at length, provided with a monumental tower and a superb light, well worthy of the position of this lonely Rock as being, from the navigator's point of view, the most important outpost of Europe".

Lloyds used Fastnet as a regular signal station from its establishment until 1920. Part of the lighthouse keeper's job was to pass on flag signals from passing ships and telegraph messages to Brow Head Signal Station on shore.

The lighthouse was unwatched on 3 April 1989 and has been operating automatically ever since. The current light character is a white flash every 5 seconds with nominal range of 27 nautical miles. The light is also exhibited by day when the fog signal is sounding. The foghorn's character is 4 blasts every 60 seconds.

The Fastnet race, held biennially by the Royal Ocean Racing Club, has become a world class event. The sailing boats sail 630 nautical miles from the Solent by the west and then turn around the Fastnet lighthouse before going back along the English coastline and arriving in Plymouth.

If you would like to see this magnificent lighthouse, take the R591 from Bantry to Goleen and then on to Crookhaven. You will need to go by boat from Crookhaven Harbour. You can also see the light by taking the ferry from Baltimore to Cape Clear Island.

Roancarrigmore and Ardnakinna

Bere Island is located 2 miles (3 km) off the coast in Bantry Bay, County Cork. The island faces the open Atlantic to the south. For many years, it was an important British military and naval base. Today, the Irish Army uses it for training. In 1847, the Admiralty recommended that a beacon should mark the western entrance to Castletownbere and an unlighted beacon on the western end of Bere Island was constructed. Today, one will find the more modern Ardnakinna lighthouse (navigational location 51° 37.1' N 9° 55' W). The current lighthouse was established on 23 November 1965 with its 66-foot (20 m) high, round white tower. Ardnakinna has a character of 2 white and 2 red flashes every 10 seconds, and a nominal range of 17 nautical miles in white and 14 nautical miles in red.

A low rock, Roancarrig, at the eastern entrance to Bantry Bay has had a lighthouse on it since 1847. George Halpin Senior, who designed the tower, chose this location instead of the eastern end of Bere Island (navigational location 51º 39.1' N 9º 44.8' W). The light, built by Mr Howard of Limerick, was established in 1847. It has a white round tower with one black band. The beacon, which flashes white and red every 3 seconds, has a nominal range of 18 nautical miles under white and 14 nautical miles under red. The lighthouse was automated on 23 September 1975.

Roancarrigmore

Roancarrigmore

Bantry Bay is a long inlet off the Atlantic Ocean and an area of outstanding natural beauty. The bay is 30 miles (48 km) long and 10 miles (16 km) at its broadest point. It is one of the largest and deepest natural bays in Europe. Bantry Bay is surrounded by mountains and separates the Beara Peninsula to the north from the Sheep's Head Peninsula to the south. The bay gives good shelter to yachts and ships in adverse weather.

Bantry Bay was twice entered by French fleets in 1689 to support James II against William of Orange. In 1796, a French invasion fleet sailed into Bantry Bay to join forces with Wolfe Tone and the United Irishmen. However, a storm changed the course of history, forcing the French to turn back to Brest. Again in 1798, a French force entered the bay in support of the United Irishmen and Wolfe Tone. This time, Tone was aboard a different ship, the *Hoche*, with the French General Jean Hardy. Tone knew the English would consider him a prisoner of war if he were captured but it was a risk Tone was willing to take.

Bantry Bay gives its name to a famous longboat that is actually of French design not Irish. Similar to a Captain's boat used two centuries ago by the navies of France, Britain, Sweden, Russia, Spain and the USA, the *Bantry Bay* boat is of fairly simple but elegant construction. She is 38 feet (12 m) long and 7 feet (2 m) on the beam and draws 14 inches (36 cm) of water. The original longboat was captured off Bear Island in Bantry Bay on Christmas Eve 1796. Built by the French Navy in Brest, the longboat is currently a central exhibit in the National Maritime Museum of Ireland.

Castletownbere is the principle town on the Beara Peninsula and it is the largest whitefish port in Ireland. The sheltered Berehaven Harbour, lying between Castletownbere and Bere Island, plays host to Irish, French, Cornish, Scottish, English, Dutch and Spanish fishing fleets, as well as the Russian and eastern European factory fishing ships and flotillas of pleasure craft. Berehaven is the second largest natural harbour in the world.

To reach the general area of these lighthouses, take the N71 toward Kenmore and turn south on the R572 at Glengarriff. Once in the area, a boat ride is necessary to see the lighthouses. For Ardnakinna, take the ferry from Castletownbere to the western end of Bere

Island. Once on the island, follow the Beara Way signs to the west and you will see the lighthouse. For Roancarrigmore, you take the ferry to Bere and walk to the east end where you will see the lighthouse in the distance.

Bull Rock

In the southwest of Ireland at the end of Beara Peninsula lies the large island of Dursey and just offshore from the island are a "herd" of islands known as Bull, The Cow, The Calf and The Heifer. As would be expected, the largest of the herd is Bull Rock. The island is 300 feet (92 m) high and 600 feet (185 m) in diameter. Heifer Rock just barely peeks its head above water and Calf Rock lies only 78 feet (24 m) above sea-level and is only one-half acre (0.2 ha) in size. Bull Rock has a tunnel large enough to accommodate a ship running through it. These rocks have always been a major threat to shipping.

It is believed that Bull Rock played an important part in the ancient history of Ireland. King Milesius of Spain was outraged at the death of his uncle, Ith, at the hands of the Irish. He sent his nine sons with a great fleet to Ireland to avenge his brother's death. On

Bull Rock

landing in Ireland, the sons of King Milesius went inland and there encountered the Kings of the Tuatha de Danann. The Spaniards demanded either kingship or battle. The Kings of the Tuatha de Danann stalled, asking for a week alone on the island to make a decision. The sons of King Milesius agreed to return to their ships and sailed a short distance off the coast of Ireland. The treacherous Tuatha de Danann then raised a great storm against the Milesian fleet, which drove them far to the west. Circling the island three times until the storm blew itself out, the Spanish fleet finally landed at the south end of the island. Here, they divided their fleet and men. Most of the sons of Milesius had been killed in the landing or during the storm. Legend says that Donn, one of the sons, died of some disease and had his body put on Bull Rock to prevent the disease from infecting more of Ireland. Heber, the eldest son, remained in the south of Ireland.

Legend also connects the "herd" of islands with Fastnet Rock. According to one particular legend, every May Day before the sun rises and the mist disappears, Fastnet Rock sets out on a journey of 20 miles (32 km) to visit its relations, The Bull, The Cow, The Calf and The Heifer. After saying "Hello", Fastnet then returns back to its home until next May Day.

The first lighthouse placed on a member of the "herd" was on Calf Rock. The builder objected to construction on Calf Rock but was told by the Ballast Board, the Admiralty and the Board of Trade to build the light anyway. The cast-iron tower was 102 feet (31 m) high. It was completed by August 1864 but the lantern and light were not exhibited until 30 June1866. Due to an error, the shutters were put inside of the tower instead of outside and in the mid-1860s the large plate glass windows of the tower were broken by a huge storm. On 20 January 1869, a storm destroyed 8 feet (2.5 m) of the tower's railings and shed. On 12 February, the worst storm struck. A mainland keeper misread the flag signals from the Calf. Thinking the keepers' lives were in danger, he, along with six other men, set out into the stormy sea to rescue the keepers. Upon arrival on the rock, they found the keepers were safe so they turned back for the mainland. Unfortunately, they never made it. They were all drowned on the return trip when the sea capsized the boat. After two years, the lighthouse was back in operation only to suffer another storm on 27 November 1881, which put the light out of commission. The ruins of the cast-iron lighthouse can still be seen today on the top of Calf Rock.

Work was begun on a new lighthouse on higher Bull Rock after the destruction of Calf Rock's light. While the construction was being carried out, a temporary light in the form of an old lightship lantern was placed on the west end of Dursey Island. In 1889, the new light was established on Bull Rock with oil-gas works, keepers' accommodation and an explosive foghorn (navigational location 51° 35.5' N 10° 18.1' W). The new light, with its 49-foot (15 m) white tower, at an elevation of 272 feet (84 m) was higher but still at risk from the sea. In 1937, the sea washed over the top of the rock and destroyed the keepers' house.

The new light functioned well but was upgraded, in April 1902, by the addition of a siren foghorn with three compression-operated trumpets. The foghorn was discontinued on 17 May 1987. In 1910, the lantern was converted to vaporised paraffin, which increased the beacon's candlepower. Another increase in candlepower occurred in August 1974 when the light was made electric. Today, the light's character is white flashed every 15 seconds with a nominal range of 21 nautical miles. Another welcome addition, in 1969, was a helipad,

which allowed the keepers to be easily moved on and off the island. The keepers' families lived near Dursey Sound to the east of Bull Rock.

To see Bull Rock lighthouse, follow the directions for Ardnakinna to Castletownbere but continue south on the R572 to Dursey Island. Once in Garnish, take the cable car to Dursey and walk to the end of the island. The remains of the temporary light that was used during the construction of Bull Rock can still be seen here. If you look straight ahead, you will see Calf Rock with its ruined lighthouse and if you turn 90 degrees you will see Bull Rock.

Skellig Michael

Since about the seventh century, a monastic compound has been perched on the steep sides of the rocky island of Skellig Michael. The island is located 8 miles (13 km) off the point of the Iveragh Peninsula, County Kerry, in southwest Ireland. Dedicated to the Archangel Michael, this location equals, if not surpasses, the two other great monastic centres in western Europe that were built in his honour: Mont St Michel in Normandy (France) and St Michael's Mount in Cornwall (England). There is a prehistoric "standing stone" with an incised Celtic cross 714 feet (220 m) above sea-level on the top of the second and highest of the two peaks of Skellig Michael. Medieval pilgrims, after visiting the monastery, would climb to the top and kiss the rock, thus proving their piety!

The extreme remoteness of Skellig Michael has until recently discouraged visitation, allowing an exceptional state of preservation. The island is almost impossible to reach safely for most of the year due to large ocean swells and crashing surf. The buildings on the island remain virtually the same as when they were first built, more than 1,400 years ago. *The Forgotten Hermitage of Skellig Michael* (Discovery Series II) tells a dramatic and stunning account of a ninth-century hermitage discovered on the South Peak of Skellig Michael. It is the story, pieced together from patchy remains, study and conjecture, of a man's attempt to live on a tiny ledge some 700 feet (215 m) above the Atlantic on the outer edge of the European landmass. "An incredible, impossible, mad place. I tell you the thing does not belong to any world that you and I have lived and worked in; it is part of our dream world,"

Skellig lighthouse

wrote George Bernard Shaw after he returned from a visit on 17 September 1910. It is considered one of the most remarkable and best-preserved archaeological sites in the British Isles.

There is no evidence that the monks who lived on Skellig tried to warn passing ships with beacons. In 1796, a request was made by the Grand Jury of the County of Kerry to have a lighthouse placed on Bray Head. Twenty years after the request, the Ballast Board, who then had responsibility for the lighthouses, finally looked into the matter. George Halpin Senior looked at the situation along that part of the coastline and recommended that two lighthouses be built on Great Skelligs Rock instead of Bray Head. In November 1820, Trinity House sanctioned the building of the two lights.

Construction could not begin until the island's owners at the time, the Butler family, got the rent they wanted. As soon as the rent was paid, Halpin designed a plan using the quay with some modification that had been in use for thousands of years. The facilities were built mostly out of rubble masonry with slate cladding on the outside walls. The cladding came from the island. One tragic result of the building was that some of the 600 steps chiselled into the rocks by the monks, worn smooth by years of storms and footsteps, were destroyed.

The lower tower was ready for its lantern in January 1826, but construction had not begun on the upper tower and Halpin refused to turn on the lower light until the upper one was completed. The upper tower was completed and both lights established on 4 December 1826, even though some work remained on the upper tower (navigational location 51° 46.2' N 10° 32.5' W). Both lights had first-order catoptric lenses. The upper light is 372 feet (114 m) above water and visible for 25 nautical miles, and the lower light visible for 18 nautical miles from its position 176 feet (54 m) above the water.

A light was established on the most westerly of the Blanket islands, Inishtearaght, 22 miles (35 km) north of Skellig. The upper light on Skellig was turned off when Inishtearaght was established. In 1904, Engineer-in-Chief C.W. Scott proposed that a more powerful light be built west of the now dark upper lighthouse. After much study, it was decided to put an explosive foghorn near the upper light and to improve the light of the lower tower. On 22 December 1909, a new optic with a third-order lens, which flashed 3 times every 10 seconds was established in the lower tower. The foghorn was established in 1914 but did not work and so the Skellig did not have a foghorn until 9 December 1914. The automatic foghorn only operated for five years until it was removed and operated manually until 1948.

In December 1951, the lantern of the lower light was flooded and extinguished for 24 hours by an enormous wave. The Tour of Inspection Committee recommended, in 1962, that consideration be given to improving the lower lighthouse. At a cost of £49,000, the 1826 tower was torn down, a new concrete 40-foot (12 m) tower built on the same spot, all dwellings redesigned and a helipad added. The new tower was 175 feet (54 m) above sea-level. The current character of the light is 3 white flashes every 10 seconds with a nominal range of 27 nautical miles. The facilities were automated and the keepers removed in March 1987. The CIL have recently decided that maintaining the diesel generators is too costly. Instead they plan to harness the power of the sun, using solar panels to store energy in batteries. The annual saving could be around £25,000.

Access is by boat from Ballinskelligs or Port Magee, opposite Valentia Island. Getting to the lighthouse is difficult, but if you climb to Christ's Saddle where the monastery is located you can see the lighthouse off to the left down the cliff. The Skellig Island Experience Visitor Centre is a good place to get information on going to the lighthouse and, indeed, the area in general. You can take their trip to Skellig to see the island. Trips generally run from late April to late September, depending on the weather. Boats generally leave at 11 am and arrive back at 4 pm, give or take half an hour.

Little Samphire Island

Little Samphire Island lighthouse is located in County Kerry. County Kerry is one of the most visited counties in Ireland and some of its attractions, such as the Lakes of Killarney and the Ring of Kerry, are world famous. Killarney National Park contains beautiful mountainous and lakeside scenery and is easily accessible from the busy tourist centre of Killarney Town. The Dingle Peninsula has some impressive forts, the largest concentration of the tiny ancient beehive huts built by Kerry's first farmers and Christian monks around the eighth century, and the most perfect of Ireland's distinctive upturned boat-shaped, oratory churches, the Gallarus Oratory. Regular boat trips leave from the bustling fishing port of Dingle Town to see Kerry's resident bottlenose dolphin, Fungi, who has become a legend in his own time.

Little Samphire Island

Little Samphire lighthouse

Kerry, in the very southern-most part of Ireland, has a reputation for warmer weather than the north of the island.

The peninsula inspired films like *Ryan's Daughter*, which tells the story of 1916 Ireland where Sarah Miles marries tweedy schoolteacher Robert Mitchum but soon begins an affair with Christopher Jones, a soldier of the occupying British Army. This film received many honours including Academy Awards in 1970.

Fenit, just 7 miles (11 km) from Tralee, is a picturesque fishing village on the shores of Tralee Bay. It is home to Tralee Sailing Club, which brings plenty of colourful activity around the coastline during the summer season. The area has good sandy beaches stretching as far as Ballybunion to the north and Dingle to the south. Fenit Beach was awarded Blue Flag status by the EU in 1999. Fishing is good, particularly for monkfish. The world record monkfish was caught off Fenit and is on display locally. Brendan the Navigator (484–577), who it is suggested may have discovered America, was born here. St Brendan is the patron saint of Kerry.

Half a mile (1 km) west of Fenit, lying half a mile offshore, is Little Samphire Island. The island is a good location for a warning device to lead ships around the dangerous outer rocks at the entrance to the bay. Tralee merchants and influential shipowners asked the Ballast Board of Dublin to build a lighthouse on the little island to make the passage to Tralee safer. The Board agreed and George Halpin Senior surveyed the area. He found that one light in the area might not be enough to light the entrance to the canal that connected the bay with the town of Tralee. After further evaluation, it was decided to build a lighthouse on the island but it took Trinity House a long time to approve the decision. The people of Tralee were annoyed at the slowness of the project as the lighthouse construction was not started until March 1849 and not finished until 1 July 1854 (navigational location 52° 16.2' N 9° 52.9' W). Red and white sectors marked the character of the fixed light. The tower was made of a natural blue limestone and had separate dwelling houses for the keepers.

In 1910, those responsible for Fenit Pier and Harbour complained to the CIL that the light was not working as well as it could be. The decision was made to change the beacon from fixed to occulting. The new character was 3 seconds dark, 3 seconds flash and 3 seconds dark. At the request of the Imperial Merchant Service Guild, the light was once again changed on 29 May 1931 with the addition of a green sector. The light was converted from oil to acetylene and the character changed from group occulting to a single flash every 5 seconds. Still the Tralee and Fenit Harbour Commissions were concerned that the light was not bright enough. The Commissioners evaluated the light and found that increased lights on the mainland in the area were interfering with the signal. The answer was to convert the light to electricity. The current character is flashing white, red and green every 5 seconds. The white flash has a nominal range of 16 nautical miles and the red/green a nominal range of 13 nautical miles. The light was automated on 2 January 1956 and the keepers removed.

If you would like to visit this tidy little lighthouse, then take the R558 from Tralee to Fenit Pier. Take the footpath along the beach until you see the lighthouse. At low tide, it is sometimes possible to walk to the lighthouse but be sure to know the tidal schedule as you could be marooned at the lighthouse by high tide.

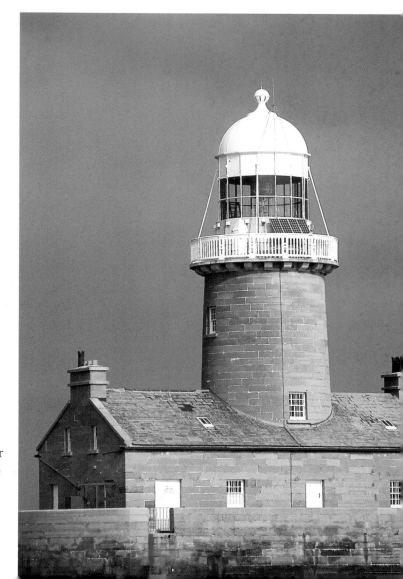

Beeves Rock light

Beeves Rock

Beeves Rock lighthouse is located in the County of Limerick. Limerick is one of Ireland's leading tourist and business centres and its most striking feature is the River Shannon, flowing majestically beneath the city's three bridges. Limerick has its origins on and around the island of Inisbhton, now known as Kings Island. Created by a loop of the River Shannon and its tributary the River Abbey, it is connected to the city mainland by four bridges: Thomond, Matthew, Baal and O'Dwyer. The Shannon tidal area, where Limerick City now stands, has been occupied since the fifth century by Christian settlements; the time of Ireland's patron saint, St Patrick, and Limerick's patron saint, St Munchin.

The Shannon Estuary Ports Commissioners, who used to be called the Limerick Harbour Commissioners, have responsibility for one of the more unusual lighthouses in Ireland. Beeves Rock lighthouse is located near the entrance of the Fergus River in the upper part of the Shannon Estuary. The

Beeves Rock Limerick Chamber of Commerce requested some type of device be placed on Beeves Rock. After much debate, a tower was completed on the rock in 1816, which would be later turned into a lighthouse. Lord Mounteagle of Mount Trechand Foynes applied to build a lighthouse on the north end of Foynes Island. The Ballast Board and the Limerick Chamber of Commerce decided that Beeves Rock would be the best position for the light (navigational location 52° 39' N 9° 1.3' W). Converting the old tower into a lighthouse did not seem feasible, so George Halpin Senior built a dark stone dwelling, which would house the keepers with a tower on top. Working time on the rock was limited because when the tide was high the rock was covered by 8 feet (2.5 m) of water. The structure was completed in 1851, but it took another four years to install the third-order dioptric lens. The light was established in May 1855. It has undergone many changes since it was established. Currently the light's character is flashing every 5 seconds white to the south with a nominal range of 12 nautical miles, and red to the north with a nominal range of 9 nautical miles.

The lighthouse was automated on 11 February 1933 and the keepers removed. Along with all the other structures in the Shannon Estuary, it is part of a new study to evaluate the tremendous scope for further industrial and commercial development of the Shannon ports industry in the estuary. The Shannon Estuary, varying from 1 to 3 miles (1.6-4.8 km) wide, is a substantial area stretching 60 miles (96 km) from Limerick to the seas. Currently, eight million tons of traffic use the estuary annually, a large proportion of which is heavy-fuel oil and it is a significant contributor to international port traffic in Ireland.

Hopefully, the expansion of the ports will not disturb some of the area's most famous residents; there are over 100 dolphins in a resident breeding group in the Shannon Estuary.

The dolphins travel within the estuary in small family groups of mainly mothers and calves. The Shannon dolphins are one of only five groups of resident dolphins in Europe.

If you would like to see the lighthouse and maybe get a peek at the dolphins, you will need to hire a boat from Foynes. Foynes in itself is worth visiting. You can find Foynes on the N69 west of Limerick. Foynes was the fulcrum point for air traffic between the United States and Europe during the 1930s and 1940s. The Foynes Museum recalls the golden age of the flying boats and includes a 1940s cinema as well as an Aviation Sculpture Park. The famous Irish coffee was invented in Foynes in 1942.

Loop Head

The Shannon River is the longest river in Ireland, rising in northwestern County Cavan and flowing for about 161 miles (257 km) in a southerly direction to enter the Atlantic Ocean via a 70-mile (112 km) estuary below Limerick City. The source of the Shannon is generally considered to be the pools at the foot of Tiltinbane Mountain. As the main river draining the central lowland of Ireland, it is surrounded by marshes and bogs for much of its course and widens at various points into lakes, many with islands.

North of the mouth of the Shannon stands Loop Head Peninsula. There are many things to do on the Loop Head Peninsula including good fishing for pollock, bass and mackerel. The coastal scenery on Loop Head is spectacular with splendid examples of cliffs, sea stacks, sea caves, chasms and rocks. The well-known "Bridges of Ross" is a sea arch formed by marine erosion. The legendary warrior Cuchulain, the most renowned of the Red Branch

*Loop Head
at dusk*

Loop Head   Knights, is supposed to have leaped from Loop Head to escape the attentions of the witch Mal, who drowned trying to follow. "Loop" is a corruption of "leap". The Kilbaha village church houses the "Little Ark", a wooden "church" built on wheels. Years ago when the celebration of mass was forbidden, the locals built the ark and when the tide was out, brought it to the beach, where the priest celebrated mass from the inside, with the people outside surrounding the ark. The beach was considered no man's land, so no interruption of the mass could occur.

Among the highlights of Loop Head Peninsula is Loop Head lighthouse. A lighthouse has been in place in this area since 1670 when Sir Robert Reading built a cottage with a platform on top for a coal burning fire. Near the current lighthouse, a small portion of the remains of the first lighthouse cottage can be seen. Due to poor management and lack of maintenance, the lighthouse fell in to disrepair and was finally discontinued. The area did not have a light for over 20 years until 1770 when the light was re-established because of the complaints from local merchants.

In 1802, Thomas Rogers replaced the cottage with a traditional white tower. Four rooms and a lantern with 12 oil lamps were contained inside the 12-foot (4 m) wide and 76-foot (23 m) high tower. The light was intensified using a 22-inch (56 cm) diameter convex lens of "bottle glass" or "bull's eye" glass. The Limerick Chamber of Commerce was worried in 1836 that the light was not bright enough, so they requested a new tower be built. The request was not granted until 1844, when George Halpin Senior designed a tower to be built by a Limerick firm. The new tower was completed and the light established on 1 May 1854 (navigational location 52° 33.7' N 9° 55.9' W). It operated as a fixed light for 15 years until an intermittent light replaced it. A screen was rotated around the light source by a clock-like machine, which had to be wound by hand. This gave a character of 20 seconds on and 4 seconds off. In 1971, the light was converted to electricity and the optic was controlled by an electric motor instead of the old clockwork rotation machine. The current character of the light is 4 white flashes every 20 seconds with a nominal range of 23 nautical miles.

   In 1977, Loop Head's radio beacon was grouped with the new radio beacon on Slyne. This was only the beginning of Loop Head becoming involved in major wireless communications. Today, Loop Head is a DGPS station. GPS is, of course, a very reliable and precise positioning system with a maximum margin of error of only 920 feet (283 m). For most mariners this was probably more than adequate, but for the military it was not good enough. Thus, a localised corrective system called Differential GPS has been developed with accuracy to within 12 feet (3.7m). Differential GPS (DGPS) is the regular Global Positioning System (GPS) with an additional correction differential signal added. This correction signal improves the accuracy of the GPS and can be broadcast over any authorised communication channel. DGPS involves the cooperation of two receivers, one that is stationary and another that is roving around making positional measurements. The stationary receiver is the key and it ties the satellite measurements into a solid local reference. Navigation is much safer and less of a hassle with DGPS. It is not only an asset for navigating ships but is useful to fishermen look-

Kilcredaune light

ing for crabs, lobsters and crawfish. Using DGPS, fishermen are able to find and drop traps into crevices barely wider than the traps themselves. This saves costly fuel, valuable time, and wear and tear on men and machinery. DGPS is also useful in locating traps after marker floats have been accidentally cut, permitting later recovery by diving at the exact location if the water is shallow enough.

   If you want to visit the lighthouse without DGPS, go to Kilkee and then south down the peninsula on the R487 towards Kilbaha. The lighthouse sits at the mouth of the Shannon.

Kilcredaune

Because of its size and the amount of traffic, the Shannon Estuary needed several lights. In 1819, the Limerick Chamber of Commerce applied to the Ballast Board for lighthouses to be placed on Scattery Island and Kilcredaune Point. Kilcredaune was well located to guide ships to the mouth of the Shannon Estuary and Carrigaholt, so it was selected as a site for a lighthouse (navigational location 52° 34.8' N 9° 42.5' W).

George Halpin Senior designed a 43-foot (13 m) solid stone tower that was painted white. The tower was connected to the keepers' accommodation by a short corridor. The lantern sits 136 feet (42 m) above sea-level. In October 1930, two vessels were wrecked on the Beal Bar and it was decided a second light was needed. The keepers were removed from Kilcredaune, and in 1941 a new truncated lantern was fitted to replace the original one. The tower was also given a flat top that looks like a Chinese hat. The light was converted to electricity in 1979. The current character of the light is a white flash every 6 seconds and a nominal range of 13 nautical miles.

The area around the lighthouse has many interesting places to visit. Carrigaholt is a rustic but popular fishing port where dab, flounder and dogfish are caught from the pier, while spinning and float anglers can catch pollock and wrasse. Conger can be hooked especially at night. In 1588, seven ships of the Spanish Armada sheltered in Carrigaholt Harbour. One of those ships was burned by the crew and allowed to sink in the estuary.

In April 1912, the Marconi Radio Company set up a station in Ballybunion. Much of the material for the new station was transported on a monorail line. The station's aerial consisted of 7 masts: the middle one was 500 feet (154 m) high, made of pinewood, and set in a concrete base whilst the other 6 were 300 feet (92 m) high. The site contained a miniature railway to take items from the powerhouse to the transmitter station. Following the first world war, Ballybunion radio station was used mainly for coastal and shipping traffic as well as for experimental purposes. In March 1919, Marconi installed a 2.5-kilowatt voice transmitter and his engineer, W.T. Ditcham, made the first east-west transatlantic radiotelephone call. He said, "Hello America. Hello, Picken. Can you hear me? This is Ditcham of Chelmsford England, speaking from Ballybunion Ireland". The other end did not have any equipment to answer but long-wave radio transmission had begun. William Ditcham continued to broadcast a regular daily programme over 12 days on a wavelength of 38,000 metres. The broadcasts were heard as far away as Louisburg, Cape Breton in Nova Scotia, Canada. In July 1922, during the Irish Civil War (1922–3), the Clifton radio station was blown up. In order to prevent a similar occurrence in Ballybunion, the radio station was dismantled and the equipment transported to Britain. Just outside the town, a large stone by the roadside marks the site of the Marconi Wireless Station.

Ballybunion has played host to holiday-makers since the early 1800s. The area has two internationally recognised Blue Flag beaches. Fine caves can be found at the south end of the beach. Dividing the main beach is a mound on which stands the wall of Ballybunion castle, once a sixteenth-century Fitzmaurice stronghold. The wall, 30 feet (9 m) high and 6 feet (2 m) thick, is pierced by 2 large holes and 5 window slits, and has become Ballybunion's trademark. A superb cliff-top walk leading around the headlands to Nun's Beach can be found above the main beach.

Ballybunion is home to a golf course ranked as one of the world's top ten. There are two great courses at the world famous Ballybunion Golf Club. The old course is the famous one but the new course, with its succession of formidable par-5s and breathtaking beauty, qualifies as one of the world's golf masterpieces.

In 1993, a scientific survey of the Shannon Estuary dolphins was carried out with the land-based observations made from Kilcredaune Head. The estuary was scanned every 30 minutes using a telescope for approximately 10 minutes. During each scan, the number and approximate sizes of any dolphins observed were recorded and assigned to an approximate location using fixed landmarks such as headlands and navigation buoys. Group size and behaviour were recorded, especially the presence of calves. One important recommendation from the study was that land observations make no or minimal intrusion on dolphins' behaviour, unlike studies carried out from boats, which may strongly influence activities. This proved it is better to go out and watch the dolphins at the lighthouse than to take the sightseeing boats, which can interfere with the dolphins' community life.

If you want to visit the lighthouse, go to Kilkee and then head south down the peninsula on the R487 until you come to the R488 where you turn south towards Carrigaholt. From Carrigaholt, follow the Loop Head Drive. The road will turn right but you should drive straight ahead towards a Swiss-looking wooden chalet, which is marked as private property. You should ask at the house if you can visit the lighthouse.

Inisheer – characteristic stone walls, with the lighthouse in the distance

Inisheer and Eeragh (Aran Islands)

Off the west coast of Ireland, plain limestone islands are criss-crossed with stone walls built over thousands of years. These are the Aran Islands. The islands are Inishmor, Inishmaan and Inisheer, or, in Irish, Inis Mór, Inis Meáin and Inis Oírr. Many pre-Christian, early Christian and medieval antiquities are found here, including the Iron Age forts at Dun Aengus on Inishmor and Dun Conchuir on Inishmaan. They are among some of the oldest ruins in Ireland although their origins remain obscure. After the Battle of Moytura, before the Christian era, it is said that many of the Firbolgs, fleeing before the conquering Dedanaans, sought and found refuge in the Aran Islands.

St Enda received a grant of land in the Aran Islands from Oengus, King of Cashel, his brother-in-law. There he founded a monastery, one of the first in Ireland, and he is considered the patriarch of Irish monks. Subsequently, this area became a part of Ireland called Munster. The islands' schools acquired such a reputation that students came from far and wide. Food produced in the islands was plentiful but the islanders must still have led a frugal life.

Inisheer lighthouse

During the Middle Ages, the islands were fought over by the O'Briens of Clare and the O'Flaherties of Galway. At the end of the sixteenth century, the English ended the dispute by building a strong fort, which later became the scene of fighting between Royalists and Roundheads, and Jacobites and Williamites, and was not evacuated for many years. While traditional Irish culture was on the wane in other parts of Ireland, the Aran Islands' relative isolation saved the language and, until recently, the style of dress. The inhabitants fished in frail currachs, small fishing boats, of laths covered with tarred canvas. Originally, hide was used to protect the people from the battering Atlantic. Scanty crops are obtained from small pockets of earth found here and there amidst the rocks. The smallholdings are sub-divided by numerous stone walls and what soil there is has been literally made by the islanders themselves. The islands have few trees but over 400 species of wildflowers have been found there.

On Inisheer, a school teaches the original Irish language, Gaelic. It is believed that Ireland has 100,000 Gaelic speakers. Of those, 50,000 use Gaelic as their first language and the 300 residents of Inisheer would be included in that group.

Several lighthouses have been built on the Aran Islands. Inishmor, the largest island, had the first one from 1818 to 1857. It was discontinued on 1 December 1857 because it was too high and fog often hid it from passing ships. It was replaced with two lighthouses, one of which is Eeragh on the small island often called the Western Island or Rock Island. Eeragh is off the northern tip of Inishmor (navigational location 53° 8.9' N 9° 51.4' W). It has a 131-foot (40 m) tower made of local limestone, which is painted with two black bands.

The tower stands 115 feet (35 m) above the water. Its light has a character of a white flash every 15 seconds with a nominal range of 24 nautical miles. The keepers were removed on 21 January 1978. A wind-powered generator manufactured by Proven Engineering Products Ltd, Kilmarnock, Scotland was installed at Eeragh, which has proved to be successful. The wind generator reduces diesel requirements and expensive shipping operations necessary for station refuelling.

The second lighthouse is on Inisheer (Island of the East), the smallest of the Aran Islands, which is only 5 miles (8 km) from the mainland. Inisheer is approximately 2.5 miles (4 km) long and 1.5 miles (2.4 km) wide. An Loch Mor (the Big Lake) takes up a large part of the island. Nearly round in appearance, Inisheer is geologically connected to the Burren. An important and strategic site for wildlife and plant life, it also boasts one of the best beaches in Clare. Like the other Aran Islands, this island is virtually pollution free.

The lighthouse service knew the light on Inisheer as South Aran (navigational location 53° 02.8' N 9° 31.5' W). It has a 112-foot (34 m) white tower with 1 black band. The beacon has an isophase character of white and red every 12 seconds. The white has a nominal range of 20 nautical miles and the red a nominal range of 16 nautical miles. The lighthouse is also a racon station. Racons, also called radar beacons, radar responders or radar transponder beacons, are receiver/transmitter transponder devices used as a navigational aid, identifying landmarks or buoys on a shipboard-radar display. A racon responds to a received radar pulse by transmitting an identifiable mark back to the radar set. The displayed response has a length on the radar display corresponding to a few nautical miles, encoded as a Morse character beginning with a dash for identification. The inherent delay in the racon causes the displayed response to appear behind the echo from the structure on which the racon is mounted.

Eeragh

Today, County Galway administers the Aran Islands and their 900 inhabitants. However, they are geologically linked to nearer County Clare. To reach the Aran Islands, there are ferryboats from Galway and Rossaveal or you can fly with Aer Arann from Connemara. If you take the ferry, you must buy a ticket to an individual island. For Inisheer, you get a yellow ticket and the lighthouse can be seen from the ferry on your left. Once on the island, you can either walk or take a pony trap or a tractor-driven tour bus to get close to the lighthouse. For Eeragh, you take the ferry to the island of Inishmor.

Blackrock Mayo

Ireland has two lighthouses with the name Black Rock; one is in County Mayo and the other is in County Sligo. Mayo's Black Rock (navigational location 54° 4' N 10° 10.2' W) is a small island off the coast with steep, high cliffs surrounded by heavy surf. The island remains inaccessible by both boat and helicopter a good deal of the time because of strong westerly winds and huge Atlantic surf. Black Rock is near the edge of the continental shelf so it is continuously beaten by the landward swell. In the days of boat reliefs, it was not uncommon for keepers going to Blackrock in late October not to be relieved until the following February or March. The Blackrock tower had the highest derrick of all the Irish lighthouses because of the difficulty of landing.

First exhibited 1 June 1864, the light stands 282 feet (87 m) above the sea, making it the second highest lighthouse in Ireland. The 50-foot (15 m) tower is built from the rock of Black Rock itself. The character of the light is a white and red flash every 12 seconds. The white flash has a nominal range of 22 nautical miles and the red's nominal range is 16 nautical miles.

Blackrock, Co. Mayo

The keepers' families lived in a house connected to the tower until 1893 when they were moved to more secure, and not so desolate, accommodation on the mainland at Blacksod. The keepers were removed from Blackrock in November 1974.

There was some consideration given to using nuclear-powered lanterns at Black Rock. After much deliberation, it was decided that the tower was too high and a new optic would lose part of its power. In 1999, a solar-powered light was finally exhibited. While the solar-powered light was being put in place a temporary light was used.

The area saw a lot of action during the second world war. In the spring of 1945, a U-1105 submarine patrolled Allied convoy routes near Black Rock. Escaping detection by an Allied destroyer patrol in April, the U-boat later discovered three British destroyers, part of the Second Division of the 21st Escort Group in the area. The submarine fired 2 acoustic torpedoes and then dived to 325 feet (100 m) to escape a counterattack. Fifty seconds passed before the first torpedo struck, with the second hitting just moments later. Thirty-two crewmen from *HMS Redmill* were lost. Another ship, the *SS Macville*, hid near Black Rock but was attacked by a German bomber. The lighthouse sustained damage from gunfire but none of the keepers were hurt.

If you would like to visit the lighthouse, go to Belmullet at the top of the Mullet Peninsula. Turn south on the R313 until you come to Blacksod. You can see the lighthouse off in the distance from the Blacksod post office. The best way to view the lighthouse is by helicopter because of its dangerous location.

Blacksod

Mullet Peninsula, its craggy edges scalloped with quiet sandy beaches and shallow bays, protrudes out into the Atlantic Ocean. The Mullet Peninsula is, in fact, almost an island, joined to the mainland only at Béal an Mhuirthead (Belmullet). The area has miles of secluded beaches and sand dunes in a 16 by 10-mile (26 by 16 km) area from Blacksod Point on the south to Erris Head in the north. Interesting coves dimple the steep rocky cliffs of Erris Head to the north and the gentler, granite slopes of Termon Hill to the south. Between those 2 extremities the land is seldom more than 100 feet (31 m) above sea-level. At Annagh Head there is a coarse-grained metamorphic rock that is 2,000 million years old. It is the oldest rock yet recorded in Ireland. The similarity of the rock type and structure

The Mullet Peninsula

Blacksod light to that of the eastern seaboard of North America, Newfoundland and Greenland has led to the conclusion that the peninsula was once joined to this land mass and then torn apart when the Atlantic opened up 200 million years ago. It is also a well-known area for many rare birds, especially on the islands of Inniskea and Innisglora, as well as the many and varied archaeological sites.

In 1817, a road was established from Castlebar through Erris, but it was not until 1823 that the first two-wheeled cart passed through Binghamstown en route to the southern extremity of the peninsula. Even today, the Mullet Peninsula is considered one of the more remote areas of Ireland with the large expanse of Blanket Bog separating it from the business centre of Ballina.

At least two Spanish Armada ships are know to have sailed into Blacksod Bay - the *La Rata Sancta Maria Encoronada* and the *Duquesa Santa Ana*. A third, the *Santiago*, foundered in Broadhaven. It is alleged that there are three Armada wrecks on the north Mayo coast and two wrecks in the Broadhaven area.

At the summit of Glosh Hill stands a signal tower, built by the British early in the nineteenth century during the Napoleonic Wars to protect the coast from attack. This began a history of towers being used to keep the area safe. From Eagle Island, situated off Doonamo Head, you can see four lighthouses. Blackrock Mayo lighthouse is 12 miles (19 km) out to sea; a lonely place for the keepers in former times. At the northern mouth of Broadhaven Bay stands Ballyglass lighthouse, which guides the boats into this bay leading to Belmullet.

The fourth lighthouse, Blacksod, is at the southeastern end of the peninsula. (navigational location 54° 5.9' N 10° 3.6' W). The building is unique among Irish lighthouses since it has a square tower with the white lantern on top and the keepers' accommodation thrusting out on either side. This style of lighthouse is sometimes called "schoolhouse". The station was built near Blacksod Pier, known locally as Termon Pier, of local reddish-grey granite in 1865. The stone was brought to the site by a tramway system. The light was established on 30 June 1866. The light's character is 2 white and 2 red every 7.5 seconds. The white has a nominal range of 12 nautical miles whilst the red has a nominal range of 9 nautical miles. In conjunction with Blackrock lighthouse, it guides ships in and out of Blacksod Bay.

On 23 March 1931, the lighthouse keepers were withdrawn and the responsibility of watching the light went to the Relief Keeper at Blackrock lighthouse. In November 1933, Blacksod had its own attendant appointed. His name was Ted Sweeney. He was the first of many generations of Sweeneys to work for the lighthouse service. Ted Sweeney was also the local postmaster and while his post office was being re-built, the mail was distributed from a room under the lighthouse tower from 1969-72.

In 1944, Ted broadcast a weather forecast that would make world history since General Eisenhower used this forecast to decide whether to make the D-Day landings in France on 6 June 1944. Most of the meteorologists had predicted a week of bad weather but Ted Sweeney at Blacksod predicted a mid-week break and so the landings were scheduled during that break.

Ted seemed to always be in the middle of historic events. In July 1969, he helped Tom McClean come ashore at Blacksod Bay. Tom McClean was the first person to row alone across the Atlantic Ocean from east to west. He took just 72 days to complete this feat. Two more lighthouses are worthy of mention before leaving this area. Clare Island is the largest (4,000 acres (1,619 ha)) and the highest (1,520 feet (468 m)) island among the 365 islands of Clew Bay. The first light is Inisgort, a harbour light in Clew Bay. The lighthouse was first established on the island in 1806, built by the Marquis of Sligo. A fire destroyed the original building but it was re-built in 1818. The light was decommissioned in 1965. The second light, Clare Island lighthouse, sits on a high, sheer cliff overlooking a magnificent coastline. The Marquis of Sligo built the light in 1806 but the Dublin Ballast Board took it over four years later. A fire destroyed the lantern and part of the tower on 29 September 1813 so a temporary light was set up until 1818 when a new light was built. In 1965, the

Blacksod

Clare Island lighthouse was decommissioned after 159 years and sold to private owners. It is presently the only lighthouse in Ireland converted into a guesthouse.

If you would like to visit Blacksod lighthouse, it can be found 12 miles (19 km) south of Belmullet on the Mullet Peninsula. The lighthouse is right on the pier so it is easy to see. To get to Clare Island, O'Malley Ferries have two ferries that service the island from Roonagh on the west coast of Ireland. There is also a ferry from Louisburgh with a 20-minute sailing time.

Eagle Island

Eagle Island, a 14-acre (5.7 ha) island, lies north of Black Rock off the Mullet Peninsula in County Mayo and only 20 miles (32 km) from the edge of the continental shelf. The location is highly exposed and totally at the mercy of severe storms. Originally, two lighthouses were built here, Eagle Island East and Eagle Island West. They were to be leading lights. If a ship's captain kept in line with the twin lights at night or the towers by day, the ship would miss Stag Rocks and the other hazards in the area. The two towers were built out of stone from the islands 132 yards (122 m) apart. The West tower's construction was delayed when a storm swept the two courses already built, along with all the building supplies, out to sea. The two lighthouses were shown for the first time on the 29 September 1835 (navigational location 54° 17' N 10° 5.5' W). Eagle Island East is 64 feet (20 m) tall and Eagle Island West is 87 feet (27 m) tall. Their lanterns were both 220 feet (68 m) above high water. The white towers had a nominal range of 20 nautical miles.

The history of the Eagle Island lights is one of constant damage and rebuilding. Just *Eagle Island* four months after the lights were turned on, Eagle Island West's lantern was hit by a rock that

shattered the glass and extinguished the light. Not only was the tower damaged but also the keepers' accommodation was also demolished. In February 1850, a vicious storm damaged both lanterns and no navigational aid remained. It took over a week until repairmen could get to the island. The keepers were able to get the lights back on in four days so that when help arrived all they had to do was replace shattered glass. On 11 March 1861, a gigantic wave stretched 220 feet (68 m) up out of the sea to strike the Eagle Island East tower. Twenty-three panes of glass and some lamps were destroyed. The tower took on so much water that the keepers had to drill holes in the walls to drain it before they could open the doors. The most devastating storm hit Eagle Island on 29 December 1894. The East keepers' accommodation was so badly smashed that the keepers' families had to seek shelter in the tower only to find that the sea had broken the lantern and water was rushing down into the tower. The families were moved ashore to Corclogh on the peninsula after this episode.

The East tower was discontinued on 1 November 1895 when a first-order lens was placed in the West tower. The West tower was unwatched in March 1988. The 1,400,000-candlepower light's character is 3 white flashes every 10 seconds. It currently has a nominal range of 23 nautical miles.

Just one event of many to demonstrate the necessity of the Eagle Island facilities occurred in November 1940 when one of the keepers spotted a tanker, *San Demetrio*. A German pocket battleship had attacked the convoy she had been part of; most of the ships were sunk. The *San Demetrio*, engulfed in flames, was able to stay afloat. The crew had abandoned the ship but later five crew members went back to put out the fire, restart her engines and head for Eagle Island. The keeper saw this and called immediately for the assistance the ships needed.

East of Eagle Island is the sister light, Broadhaven (navigational location 54° 16' N 9° 53.3' W). Located on the northern tip of the Mullet Peninsula, its main purpose is to guide ships around a sunken rock and up a channel to Belmullet. The white tower stands 50 feet (15 m) tall. The night character is isophase white and red every 4 seconds. The white light has a nominal range of 12 nautical miles while the red has a nominal range of 9 nautical miles. It was electrified in 1977 and the keepers removed on 31 November 1931.

If you would like to visit Eagle Island you need a boat or a helicopter. If you are driving, head west from Bulmullet, turn north and then northwest. You should be able to see the lighthouse from the shore.

Metal Man and Oyster Island

Sligo Bay is the nearest neighbour to New York City on Irish shores. It is also the longest section of Ireland to face north. Sligo is the main town on the bay with a population of 17,250. Bay traffic, while modest in national terms, has remained reasonably stable over recent years and continues to make an important contribution to the economic activity of the northwest region. The cargoes are largely of coal, slack, coke and timber.

Oyster Island, with its distinctive lighthouse and five cottages, lies a short distance across the channel from Rosses Point. The island derives its name from the profusion of oyster beds that existed along its shores until the turn of the century. Separating Oyster Island

Oyster Island from Coney Island is Shrunamile, the channel of a thousand currents. Shrunamile is a suitable name because of the multitude of eddies with their peculiar whispering sound that changes with the ebb and flow of the tide. On 1 August 1837, two lighthouse towers were established on Oyster Island. They were intended to be leading lights into the port of Sligo but did not function properly. In February 1891, a temporary light replaced the discontinued old towers. In 1893, a new light was built on the northwest point of the island after the old towers were torn down (navigational location 54° 18.1' N 8° 34.2' W). The light was established in 1893. It has a 40-foot (12 m) tower that stands 43 feet (13 m) above the sea. Its light has the character of occulting white every 4 seconds with a nominal range of 10 nautical miles.

At the entrance to Sligo Harbour stands a unique navigational aid, Metal Man. (navigational location 54° 18.2' N 8° 34.5' W). By all definitions, it is a lighthouse but it is unique in structure. The Metal Man was originally cast to stand on a tower where the Blackrock Sligo lighthouse is now situated. In 1814, the original Blackrock Sligo tower was destroyed in a violent gale. Two years later in 1816, after the pleadings of the merchants of Sligo, Ballina and Killala, the tower was replaced. Fearing the replacement tower might also be destroyed, the decision was made to build a more substantial tower and the task was given to a local Ballina builder by the name of Thomas Hamm, who in 1816 constructed a 51-foot (16 m) limestone tower on Black Rock. Metal Man was originally intended to go on this tower.

The first Metal Man was exhibited in London in 1819. Records show that Thomas Kirke cast four identical models in the same year. Besides the one in Sligo Bay, one stands on a headland near Tramore beach in County Waterford. No details are available as to where the other two are located.

Perch Rock has wrecked many ships entering the port. This rock, which is clearly visible at lower points of the tide, lies between Rosses Point and Coney Island. Local Sligo shipowners petitioned to have the Metal Man placed upon this rock instead of Blackrock tower, and a proper lighthouse erected on Black Rock further out in the bay. Their efforts were successful, and Thomas Hamm erected a 15-foot (4.6 m) limestone base on which to place the Metal Man.

Metal Man

The Metal Man stands with a right arm outstretched, pointing towards the safe channel to the town of Sligo. Dressed in the blue jacket and white trouser uniform of a Royal Navy Petty Officer, he stands 12 foot (3.7 m) high and weighs 7 tons. A navigational light is mounted on a pedestal in front of him, and in the darkness ships keep this light to starboard when passing upriver.

The Metal Man acts as a leading light. Ships' captains know that their approach is correct if Metal Man is lined up with the light on Oyster Island. The Metal Man's first light was added in 1908 and powered by acetylene. It was converted to propane gas in 1979. The light at Metal Man has a character of a white light flash every 4 seconds with a nominal range of 7 nautical miles.

There are many stories and anecdotes relating to the Metal Man. Some say he is the only man from Rosses Point never to have told a lie. Some swear to have seen him come ashore to fetch a loaf of bread. A favourite is that his tunic is buttoned incorrectly because he was in a hurry to get to work as a ship was approaching the rocks.

One true story tells of how a 6,000-ton Greek steamship was entering the harbour in the 1920s to moor at the buoys under the now derelict Elsinore House. Suddenly a dense fog blanketed the area. The ship's crew, having taken their posts, were frightened when beside the starboard bow a giant appeared. The entire forward crew fled in terror and refused to return to the ship's bow until the Metal Man was explained to them.

Henry Middleton, the uncle of the poet W.B. Yeats and the painter Jack Yeats, owned Elsinore House. The Metal Man has been depicted in poem and painting by W.B. and Jack Yeats who often visited the area.

To see the Metal Man, you take the R291 north of Sligo to Rosses Point. You can see him standing in the bay. Oyster Island can be seen off to your left at the end of Rosses Point Road.

Blackrock Sligo

The first lighthouse on Black Rock in Sligo Bay was an unlit beacon of solid limestone completed in 1819. Built by Thomas Hamm of Ballina, it was to guide ships into the ports of Killala and Sligo. The station was destroyed by a storm in the autumn of 1814. Local merchants and shipowners urged that the light be re-built. In 1816, unsuccessful attempts were made to restore the light. In 1819, Thomas Hamm built a 51-foot (16 m) tower out of solid limestone on the base of the old beacon tower (navigational location 54° 18.4' N 8° 37.0' W). The tower got a new beacon in 1835 and was converted to a lighthouse. A spiral staircase went up to an entrance above the high-water mark.

In 1853, outside panniers were added to the tower, making Blackrock Sligo one of a kind. A bedroom and storage space was contained in each pannier, as there was no room in the tower for them. The panniers were built on cast-iron brackets that jutted out from the tower near the entrance level about 40 feet (12 m) above the water. The panniers were removed and the light was converted from oil to acetylene gas when the tower was demanned on 29 November 1934. The light was converted to electricity in 1965. The current tower has a day mark of white with a black band and its night character is a white flash every 5 seconds. The lighthouse's nominal range is 13 nautical miles. An auxiliary light flashes over

Blackrock Sligo

Wheat and Seal Rocks with a red flash every 3 seconds and a nominal range of 5 nautical miles.

It is believed that W.B. Yeats wrote a poem about the Blackrock lighthouse entitled the *The Black Tower*. This was his last poem, written in 1939 a week before he died.

> Say that the men of the old black tower,
> Though they but feed as the goatherd feeds,
> Their money spent, their wine gone sour,
> Lack nothing that a soldier needs,
> That all are oath-bound men:
> Those banners come not in.
>
> There in the tomb stand the dead upright,
> But winds come up from the shore:
> They shake when the winds roar,
> Old bones upon the mountain shake.

The reference to the "tomb with the dead upright" is based on a legend of a warrior king who is buried standing up near the lighthouse.

Situated 4.5 miles (7 km) from the nearest point on the mainland shore, beyond Roskeeragh Point and not too far from Black Rock, is the island of Inishmurray. Only 1 mile (1.6 km) long and 0.5 mile (0.8 km) across at its widest part, the island rises only 70 feet (22 m) above sea-level at its highest point on the western end and slopes to sea-level on the east. It is not known when Inishmurray was first settled. Over 2,000 years ago, it is said, sun worshippers gathered here. The altar of Cloch Breaca (the Speckled or Carved Stones) dates from pagan times. At one point, the island could have been home to the Formorian sea marauders who lived on Ireland's offshore islands. The island was continuously inhabited from the sixth century until 1948, although the population has fluctuated much through the years.

Until British forces set up a barracks in 1836 on the island, Inishmurray was always an independent "kingdom" ruled by its own king and queen. Conflict developed over the payment of taxes with the reigning king arguing that the mainland provided them with no business or support. The islanders made their own roads and tended to their own poor so it was felt they should not have to pay taxes to an alien authority. The island was finally evacuated of its remaining population of only 46 people in 1948. The island is now a bird sanctuary and is best known for its colony of 100 or so breeding pairs of eider ducks.

One of the finest and oldest monastic settlements in Ireland is on Inishmurray. No excavation has taken place and most of the features are extremely difficult to date but it is believed that the monastery was founded by St Molaise in the sixth century and was one of the first to be raided by the Vikings in the eighth century. The Cashel contains a number of holy sites, including Teampall na Tine (the Temple of Fire). Around the island are a series of sacred stones and wells that have been the focus of spiritual devotions since recorded time. It is believed St Columba (AD 521-97) once retreated to the islands to do penance for his sins. St Molaise advised him to go to Scotland to convert the Scots. St Columba obeyed and he founded the monastery on Iona, a Scottish Hebridean Island, in AD 563.

Despite its sacred background, Inishmurray has also been involved in some dishonest operations. In 1924, the largest quantity of illegal alcohol ever captured in the Sligo area was discovered on Inishmurray Island. A party of civic guard accompanied by the military made a lightning raid on the island early in the morning. The scene was described as a "small distillery". The distillers were taken completely by surprise and one still was discovered in actual working order, while there was only a very poor attempt made to conceal the immense quantity of wash.

If you would like to visit Blackrock Sligo, take the R291 north of Sligo to Rosses Point. After you pass Oyster Island on your left go another 0.5 mile (0.8 km) to where the road curves sharply to the right. Turn left at the big hotel and you will see the lighthouse out in the bay. If you want a closer look, you will need to get a boat at Rosses Point.

St John's Point and Rotten Island

St John's Point

County Donegal is 68 miles (109 km) long and 44 miles (70 km) wide bounded on the west and north by the ocean, on the east by Londonderry and Tyrone, and on the south by Roscommon and the bay of Donegal. Located at the mouth of Donegal Bay in the northwest of Ireland and surrounded by the Blue Stack mountains, the area has a rugged beauty and an air of mystery. From Slieve League, the highest sea cliffs in Europe, to golden sandy beaches, the region provides activities ranging from water sports to extraordinary country strolls.

St John's Point Light

Donegal Town dates back to Viking times when they built a fortress at the mouth of the River Eske. Legend says that the Viking occupation gave the town and ultimately the county its name: Dun na nGall, meaning "Fort of the Foreigners". Donegal was the family seat of the O'Donnells, chieftains of Tír Chonaill. The King of Tír Chonaill had a Norman-style tower house, O'Donnell's Castle, constructed on the banks of the Eske River in 1603.

County Donegal has more jobs and income from fishing than any other county in Ireland. Important County Donegal fishing ports are Burtonport, for many years the best wild salmon port in Europe, and Greencastle, the most important whitefishing port in Ireland north of Castletownbere. Killybegs, Ireland's premier fishing port situated on a fine natural harbour on the northern shore of Donegal Bay, is one of five ports designated as Fishery Development Harbours by the Irish Government in 1968. The town has turned its location to its advantage and over the years has built a strong shore-based support sector for the fishing industry, including boat building and repair, electronics, hydraulics, marine engineering and fabrication, net making and repair, water purification and waste treatment. It has a vibrant fish processing and export sector with a turnover of more than £110 million per annum.

In order for ships to get to Killybegs, they must pass St John's Point on the north shore of Donegal Bay. Mariners felt it necessary to place a lighthouse at St John's Point to assist the ships into Killybegs Harbour entrance by Rotten Island. It was believed that a second light was needed on Rotten Island. St John's light, designed by George Halpin Senior and built of cut granite painted white, cost £10,000 to build. It was established on

N

S

Rotten Island 4 November 1832 (navigational location 54° 34.2' N 8° 27.6' W). The tower was 50 feet (15 m) high and stood 98 feet (30 m) above the water. A first-order fixed catoptric light was installed. In 1932, it was necessary to replace the first lens with an occulting light and then in July 1942 the light was changed to flashing. The current light has a character of a white flash every 6 seconds. The lighthouse has a nominal range of 14 nautical miles.

 The second light in the area on Rotten Island was established on 1 September 1838 and had a third-order catoptric lens with a fixed white light (navigational location 54° 36.9' N 8° 26.3' W). George Halpin Senior designed it and once again used cut granite painted white. There was a tragic accident during construction when three construction staff drowned on 15 September 1836. In December 1910, the light was changed from fixed to flashing. This still did not provide enough light so in 1959 it was changed to acetylene, which gave the white beam 2,600 candlepower and 500 in red. Still not powerful enough, electricity was installed in February 1963 and the candlepower was increased to 13,000 in white and 2,600 in red. Currently the light flashes white and red every 6 seconds with a nominal range of 15 nautical miles in white and 11 nautical miles in red.

 If you want to visit the lighthouse, take the N56 west from Donegal. When you come to the Castlemurray House Hotel near Dunkineely, turn left and follow the road to the end of the peninsula. For Rotten Island, take the road to Donegal Town past the Fish Meal plant and turn right after the bridge and follow the twisting road until you reach the point overlooking Rotten Island.

Tory Island

Tory Island is located north of the section of Donegal coast known as "The Bloody Foreland". The island's nearest neighbours to the north are the Scottish Hebrides. The island gets it name from the "tors" or pillars, which are great cliffs that have been formed in a packed line. Tory only has two tiny towns, West Town and East Town.

The Harbour Commissioners and Merchants of Sligo requested a lighthouse in April *Tory Island*
1828. The Ballast Board approved it in November and the Statutory Sanction was received
from Trinity House in December 1828. George Halpin Senior designed the large station with
its 89-foot (27 m) tower, 131 feet (40 m) above high water. The light was established on 1
August 1832 (navigational location 55° 16.4' N 8° 14.9' W). A dioptric lens with a multi-
wick oil lamp replaced the original oil lamps and reflectors in 1862. In 1887, a small coal
gasworks was built at the lighthouse to replace the original fuel of oil and the lens was
changed to revolving thus giving a flashing character. A foghorn was added as well but discontinued in August 1994.

Gas was used until 1932 when it was replaced by paraffin. Electricity was brought to
the lighthouse in 1972. The current night character is 4 flashes white every 30 seconds. It has
a nominal range of 27 nautical miles. Its day mark is a black tower with a white band. The
keepers were removed and the station automated in March 1990.

Tory Island holds a special place in Celtic legend. Fable states the island was the
home of the Fomorians, the first residents of Ireland, and probably gets its name from
toiridhe meaning robber or pirate. Fifty in number, they were descendant's of the Biblical
Noah. They all perished in the great flood save one who turned into a salmon. The Fomorians were regarded as the embodiment of evil, monstrous and hideous. The most famous was
the Cyclops Balor of the Evil Eye also known as the Celtic God of Darkness. His eye was at
the back of his head. On the east coast of the island can be found the ruins of Balor's Fort. In
the heart of the island is a crater that none of the locals will approach at dark because it
makes the god angry. Also in the centre of the island is a wishing stone. If you walk around it
three times your wish will be granted. Legend says that the wishing stone was used to defeat
the British gunboat *Wasp* sent to collect taxes from the islanders. The ship was caught in a
sudden storm and all crew members drowned. The islanders have not paid taxes since.

Tory Island St Columba landed on the island in the sixth century with the help of a member of the Duggan family. The saint made the helper king of the island. The line has been unbroken ever since. The current king is Patsy Dan Rodgers who runs a pub on the island.

Some relics remain from St Columba's time, of which the most famous is the Tau Cross. It is a T-cross of Egyptian origin and is only one of two such crosses in Ireland. It has been relocated from where it was found and set in concrete on Camusmore Pier in West Town. There are other broken crosses and some carved stones scattered around the island. For a thousand years, the monastery founded by St Columba flourished until it was sacked by the Elizabethans. The ruins are mostly in the west of Tory. Of the five churches recorded in the Middle Ages, only the ruins of one remain.

Times were not always easy for the islanders whose main language is their own version of Irish Gaelic. Poitín, an illegal liquor (pronounced por-cheen), used to be brewed in the locals' homes so they had plenty of liquid refreshment to keep them warm. Since shipwrecks are frequent in the area, the islanders often benefited from the bounty. One unique find was the body of an elephant that probably died on a boat and was thrown overboard. The carcass bloated and floated on to the shore of Tory. The Donegal County Council gave the islanders concrete to build an above-ground grave for the poor creature. It is rumoured that the elephant's vault took a long time to build but the island houses had a lot of concrete added to them.

The island is famous for a boat built there. A hybrid-type currach appeared on Tory at the end of the last century when a resourceful fisherman is thought to have copied aspects of visiting yachts. A Tory currach was deposited with the National Museum in 1921. The boat is very sturdy. Gunwales are made of a number of sections joined with clenched copper and galvanised boat nails while the ribs are made of oak. The stringers running fore and aft are of ash. The covering is 18-ounce cotton duck canvas treated with coal tar. A keel is placed over the finished boat and shod with steel band. Two bilge runners are also fitted.

Tory's painters have become renowned. They started painting local scenes in a distinctive style, in 1968, after Tory fisherman John Dixon bet a visiting English painter, Derek Hill, that he could paint better pictures of local scenes. You can see the Tory Island painters' work in the community hall in West Town. One of John Dixon's best paintings of Tory is at Glebe House on the mainland.

Bird watching on Tory Island is exceptional. You will find fulmar, shag, black-headed gulls, common gulls, herring gulls, kittiwake, little terns, guillemots, razorbills, black guillemots and puffins. The corncrake is almost extinct on the mainland but some pairs can be found on the landward side of Tory Island.

Ferries serve Tory Island from four ports during the summer: Downings, Dunbeg, Magheraroarty and Portnablagh. Tory Island has just added a new airstrip. Once on the island, it is a 30-minute walk from West Town to the lighthouse.

Fanad Head

The Fanad Peninsula lies between Lough Swilly and Mulroy Bay on the north coast of County Donegal. The peninsula is a slow-moving area with lots of lovely walks. One of the most popular walks is to the saddle between Callaghpatrick (741 feet (228 m)) and the main ridge. If you follow the obvious vertical slab of rock up onto the ridge, you can reach the summit of Cnoc Colbha (1,190 feet (366 m)). The gentle ridge affords excellent views of the magnificent golden sands of Portsalon and Ballymastocker Bay. If you travel southwards, the views extend north to Fanad Head lighthouse. Continuing on to the lighthouse, you will come across a holy well covered with offerings and an impressive cliff arch called the Great Arch.

Fanad Head lighthouse sits on the end of the peninsula on the western shore. Because of its location it can safeguard ships in the North Atlantic and the entrance to Lough Swilly. It was built as a sea light and established on 17 March 1817 (navigational location 55° 16.6' N 7° 37.9' W). The design was by George Halpin Senior. He used a design similar to those at Mutton Island and Roche's Point.

The lighthouse was built as a result of the *Saldana* being wrecked on the treacherous rocks below the Head with all lives lost. The only survivor was a parrot, which was identified by a silver collar with the name of the ship on it. The Dublin Ballast Board recommended that the lighthouse be built after being petitioned to do so by Captain Hill of the Royal Navy stationed at Londonderry. He said, after sailing the northwest coast from Lough Foyle to Blacksod Bay many times, that he felt the *Saldana* would not have been lost had Fanad Head been lighted.

A larger and higher tower, and new buildings were constructed in the 1880s at Fanad Head lighthouse. The new tower was built close to the old tower. On 1 September 1886, a new light went into operation. Currently, the tower is 72 feet (22 m) high and stands 128 feet (39 m) above the water. Its day mark is a white tower and its light's characteristic is 5 white and red flashes every 20 seconds. The white light has a nominal range of 18 nautical miles and the red 14 nautical miles.

One light still did not seem to be enough and two more lights were placed in the area in 1876. One was built on Dunree Head (navigational location 55° 11.9' N 7° 33.2' W) and the other on Buncrana Pier (navigational location 55° 7.6' N 7° 27.8' W). Buncrana Pier is a 17-foot (5 m) column with an isolating character of white and red every 4 seconds. It has a nominal range of 14 nautical miles in white and 11 nautical miles in red. Dunree Head has a 20-foot (6 m) tower attached to a house. It flashes 2 times white and red every 5 seconds. Its nominal range is 12 nautical miles in white and 9 miles in red.

Many historic events involving famous Irishman have happened in the area of the Fanad Peninsula. The best known is the Flight of the Earls. In September 1607, a French ship sailed from the northern harbour of Rathmullan in Lough Swilly. On board were Hugh O'Neill, Earl of Tyrone, and Rory O'Donnell, Earl of Tyrconnell, together with more than 90 of their family and followers. Both men were Ulster chiefs who fought against Elizabeth I until their final submission in 1603. Although pardoned, they found the increasing English intervention an intolerable challenge to their traditional jurisdiction. Their ship was bound for Spain, but fierce storms forced them to disembark in France in early October. Thereafter, they made their way to Rome, where they remained in voluntary exile and where O'Neill died in 1616. Their flight left Ulster open to settlement by the Scots and English.

Rathmullan Pier is also famous for being the place from which the English kidnapped the Irish leader Red Hugh O'Donnell and shipped him off to a Dublin jail after tricking him to come aboard their ship on peaceful terms in 1587.

Another famous Irishman, Theobald Wolfe Tone, was captured in the area. He was born in Dublin in 1763. He was educated at Trinity College Dublin and in London. The young Tone often spent time in the public galleries of The Irish House of Commons. The liberal, tolerant Tone realised that the only real future for the people of Ireland was in the separation of the

Fanad Head two countries. Tone explained his actions as follows: "To subvert the tyranny of our execrable Government, to break the connection with England, the never failing source of all our political evils, and to assert the independence of my country, these were my objects. To unite the whole people of Ireland, to abolish the memory of past dissentions, and to substitute the common name of Irishman in place of the denominations of Protestant, Catholic and Dissenter; these were my means".

Tone convinced France to help his cause. The first ships were turned back in Bantry Bay by a storm but a second force under General Humbert with 1,000 men landed in August 1798. After some initial successes, Humbert surrendered to superior English forces. A further expedition of 3,000 under Generals Bompard and Hardy set sail for Ireland with Tone himself on board. They approached Lough Swilly on the north coast near Fanad Head Peninsula where an English fleet waited. The French were outnumbered and outgunned. Knowing the fate that lay in store for Tone, the French put a boat at his disposal to escape but he declined with these words, "Shall it be said that I fled while the French were fighting the battle of my country?" After a gallant battle, the French surrendered and Wolfe Tone was captured.

If you would like to visit the Fanad Head lighthouse, take the R245 north from Letterkenny until you come to the R246 to Portsalon. From Portsalon, you should travel north towards the head of the peninsula.

Inishtrahull

The most northerly island of Ireland, Inishtrahull, is a small, interesting place. The island is about 1 mile (1.6 km) in length, somewhat hour-glass in shape, with hills forming the east and west ends joined by a narrower, low stretch of ground. It marks the northern entrance to the North Channel, which leads into the Irish Sea - the major sea link between Great Britain and Ireland.

Geologists believe that this is the oldest stretch of land in Ireland. A lot of controversy has surrounded the rock that makes up this island since it has been determined that it is not made of the same material as the rest of Ireland. The rock was believed to be Lewisian

Inishtrahull, Co. Donegal

Gneiss, uncommon in this area but found on the Hebridean Islands in Scotland. After much research, it was found to be the same rock as on the Hebridean Islands of Islay and Colonsay. However, the big surprise was that it was the same as that of Greenland. After further research, it was established that the island's geological history was entwined with that of the southern tip of Greenland and not of Ireland.

This ancient piece of rock is home to the newest lighthouse in Ireland, built on 8 October 1958 by Collen Brothers (navigational location 55° 25.8' N 7° 14.6' W). This massive automated lighthouse is located at the west end of Inishtrahull. The white tower of this modern facility is 76 feet (23 m) tall and sits 194 feet (60 m) above the high-water mark. The tower's design is distinctive in that the foghorn was placed above the lantern room. The light's cur-

rent night character is flashing white 3 times every 15 seconds and has a nominal range of 25 nautical miles. Late in 2000, the Commissioners began the installation of solar power on the Inishtrahull facility and it is currently under a temporary light until the construction is completed.

The current lighthouse is actually the second lighthouse to stand on the island. The first was built at the east end of the island in 1813. George Halpin Senior designed this lighthouse for the Ballast Board of Dublin. The Royal Navy, which was using Lough Foyle as their North Atlantic base operations, requested that a lighthouse be built. The Halpin lighthouse had many changes in its light sources. The first character was a revolving light every 2 minutes. In 1864, a more modern first-order dioptric apparatus and new lantern were installed with a character of 1 flash every 2 minutes. The character was changed to 1 flash every minute in 1873 but only remained that way a short time because it was found to be similar to the Scottish lighthouse Skerryvore, 61 miles (98 km) to the north. The new character was 1 flash every 30 seconds after the change.

In 1905, a foghorn was installed at the west end of the island. Some felt it was confusing having the foghorn on one end of the island and the lighthouse on the other. The CIL decided that when it came time to update the foghorn and the lighthouse, all aids should be in one place. So the modern, unusual looking lighthouse was built.

One of the keepers, Donal O'Sullivan, became a successful writer of poetry, short stories and newspaper columns. His poem Dawn in Inishtrahull really captures the mood of the facility:

The moon shines on the Isle of Inishtrahull,
Bejewelling nuptial tinted herring gull,
May-fly dancing in the balmy air,
And moth returning to its daylight lair.

A shoal of herring breaking out at sea
Sparkle like hoar-frost on an aspen tree,
Spindrift in the shaded rocky cleft,
And raised-beach quartz that the ice-ages left.

The droning beetles seek the crevassed walls
To dive into when hungry lapwing calls;
Earwigs, likewise, into earthed homes,
And red-ants under scarred lichened stones.

An otter seeking rest on rock remote
Glistens with phosphorescence on his coat,
The snail Arborum, with his watery glue,
And bunch of pearlwort in a crystal dew.
The flaming sun ascends o'er Cantyre's Mull,
Flings out his arms, day breaks on Inishtrahull!

Uninhabited since 1928, except for visiting lighthouse personnel, there are ruined cottages and lazy beds, some rabbits, a herd of deer, and a significant breeding Eider population. The deer made news in 2000 as a daring four-hour rescue operation was launched to save six red deer from a watery grave. The deer, including two stags, two does and two fawns jumped into the sea from Inishtrahull after a crowd of 300 people descended on the island for a special open air anniversary mass. They were quickly swept 5 miles (8 km) out to sea. With just their antlers as guides, the rescuers braved treacherous waters in a Rigid Inflatable Boat (RIB) to pull the terrified animals to safety. They were able to pull the two fawns from the water first and tied their legs together in the boat. They then caught the two does, the larger of which was frightened and aggressive. With their boat full to capacity, the men radioed the Malin Coastguard for help in removing the two stags from the water. The RIB crew even held the antlers of one of the stags as he began to weaken in the water and appeared to be in danger of drowning. Tragically, the larger stag died of exhaustion before he made it on board. Once returned to their island home, the deer recovered quickly from their ordeal and disappeared from view.

If you would like to see the lighthouse, Norsemaid Sea Enterprises Ltd in Newtownards has boats taking divers out to the islands and you might be able to hitch a ride. Newtownards is east of Belfast on the A20.

Maidens Lighthouse

In 1819, the merchants and shipowners of Larne conducted a campaign to have a lighthouse placed on the Maiden Rocks. About 6 miles (10 km) north-east of Larne are the two rock islets in the North Channel know as The Maidens. The two rocks stick up about 25 feet (8 m) above the water. Also about 1.5 miles (2.5 km) north are the Allan, Highland and the Russell, extremely dangerous small islets that lie just above the water level at low tide. To add to the difficulty, treacherous reefs surround two of the islets, East Maiden and Allan.

The Corporation for Preserving and Improving the Port of Dublin gave in to pressure from the Larne shipowners and merchants and agreed

Maidens

to build two lighthouses on the Maidens in the first part of the nineteenth century. Two lights only 824 yards (761 m) apart would be built. The one on the northern-most rock would be called the West Tower or West Maiden and the one on the south rock would be called the East Tower or East Maiden. Standing 84 feet (26 m) above high water, the West Tower had a nominal range of 14 nautical miles. The East Tower sits 95 feet (29 m) above the high-water level and is 76 feet (23 m) tall. The lights were exhibited on 5 January 1829. An auxiliary light was added in 1889 to the window of the East Tower so that it would cover Highland and Russell Rocks. Its day character was 1 red flash every 5 seconds. On 12 March 1903, a new optic was installed in the East Tower (navigational location 54° 55.7' N 5° 43.6' W) and the West Tower discontinued. The current Maidens lighthouse's day mark is a white tower with a black band and its light's character is 3 white flashes every 20 seconds. It has a nominal range of 24 nautical miles. The station is also a Racon facility.

The lighthouse is located off Larne in County Antrim. Larne's motto – "Falce Marique Potens" – means "Industry by land and sea", and illustrates Larne's importance as a port for passengers and trade. The Port of Larne Harbour provides frequent ferry sailings to Scotland and England, offering passenger, car and commercial freight services.

Inland from Larne, the next impressive stretch of water is Lough Neagh, the largest body of freshwater in the British Isles. Antrim town, after which the county is named, is situated on the north-east corner of Lough Neagh. An ancient monastic monument may be seen within walking distance of the town centre. The tower here is not surrounded by rough seas and dangerous rocks, but meadow and woodland. This round tower was a place of refuge or storage, not a warning to shipping, although it might seem so on a misty day. At 93ft (28 m) high and 50ft (15 m) round at its base, the tower compares favourably with many of the Irish lighthouses. It may have been built over a thousand years ago, when shipping and international commerce were not conducted in as peaceful and civilised a manner as they are today. The only shipping Antrim's round tower would have been a warning to (or against) would have been Viking raiders.

There is a rock nearby, notable for its history rather than any danger it poses to shipping. A large rock with two hollows on its flat upper face, it may have been used in early Christian rites, such as baptism or confirmation, or for the monks to prepare their grain for baking. The most colourful and least easily proven theory is that a local witch jumped or was thrown from the top of the tower: as she fell, her elbow and knee hit the stone with such force that the impressions remain, over a thousand years later. The fact that the stone is 40 m or more from the tower gives the stone its local name - the witch's stone.

Two natural attractions of County Antrim are the Glens of Antrim and the Giants Causeway. Along the Antrim Coast Road are the nine Glens of Antrim. The glens are beautiful lush green, wooded and bog-land valleys that stretch down to the sea between rugged headlands. Quaint, tiny villages are scattered all along the coast like Ballygally, Glenarm, Cushendall and Cushendun to name but a few.

The Giants Causeway is the only UNESCO World Heritage site in Ireland and is often described as the eighth wonder of the world. William Makepeace Thackery said of it "When the world was moulded and fashioned out of formless chaos, this must have been the bit over - a remnant of chaos". The causeway is a unique formation of hexagon-shaped basalt columns, which were formed by volcanic activity in the area thousands of years ago. In the area are also beautiful columns set into the cliffs, which look like the pipes of a church organ. The causeway forms part of the Ulster Way (a walkway across Northern Ireland), with a beautiful 5-mile (8 km) cliff walk around the area.

If you would like to visit the area and the Maidens lighthouse, the best way is by boat from Larne Harbour. Larne can be found north of Belfast on the A8. You can sometimes see the Maidens lighthouse from the ferries entering or leaving Larne Port.

Mew Island light

Mew Island and Donaghadee

The Copeland Island group lies 2 to 3 miles (3-5 km) north of Donaghadee. These three islands have been responsible for as many wrecks as anywhere on the Ulster coast. Situated at the southern entrance to Belfast Lough, it is where the strong tides of the North Channel come into conflict with those swirling around the lough. These tides are called *Ramharry Race*, which means "rough and strong" in Scandinavian.

The Vikings used these islands as a base and named them Kaupmennayer - anglicised and shortened to "Copman" meaning "Merchant Isles". It is believed that St Ninian and St Launas of Bangor Abbey both visited the islands. St Ninian gave his name to the Ninion Bushes, a shoal reef on the seaward side of the islands with its warning buoy. The Copeland family, originally Norman, have had connections with the area since 1183.

Copeland Island itself is the largest island of the group and closest to the shore, the others being Mew Island and Lighthouse Island. Bleak by most standards, the island is grassy and bracken covered in parts. There are a number of holiday homes on Copeland, and a sandy beach on the southwest and Deer Bay on the northeast. Grey and Common Seals are both found, the former on

Donaghadee lighthouse and lifeboat

Copeland itself and the latter favouring the more exposed channel between Mew and Lighthouse Islands.

Lighthouse Island lies 1 mile (1.6 km) north of Copeland. The larger and higher of the two outlying islands, it has been called Laune (most likely named after St Launas), Cross, St John's or Old Lighthouse Island. It had early monastic dwellers. A cross, it is said, once stood on the island reflecting its religious connections. The National Trust owns the island where they have established a bird observatory.

Around 1711, a coal beacon was established on what was called at the time Lesser Copeland Island. Four cottage-type lights were established around Ireland at that time; the others being Old Head of Kinsale, Loop Head and Howth Head. A 6-foot (2 m) round oil lantern was placed on a 40-foot (12 m) high tower in 1796. When the Corporation for Improving the Port of Dublin known as the Dublin Ballast Board took over the operation of the lighthouses, one of the first stations they evaluated was Copeland. A new 52-foot (16 m) tower was designed by George Halpin Senior and built beside the old tower. Approximately131 feet (40 m) above sea-level, the new light had a fixed oil-powered light. It was established on 24 January 1815. The old lighthouse was used for a huge fog bell in 1851. The bell was run by a weight-driven machine, which was periodically wound up by the keepers. Ruins from the first lighthouse, the keepers' accommodation and the beacon tower can still be seen on the island.

The Belfast Harbour Commission requested that the light be moved from its current position to Mew Island. Apparently, many wrecks were actually caused by the light on Lighthouse Island being clearly seen but low lying Mew being totally overlooked. An example of such an incident occurred on 6 July 1847 when the *Sea King*, a paddle steamer, was plying the ferry trade between Belfast and Liverpool and ran aground on the eastern end of Mew Island. It was impossible to save her and she rolled over, filled with water and sank, but there was no loss of life. On 30 March 1850, the *Theresa Jane* was only one of a number of ships lost in a horrible storm. She went onto the rocks of Mew Island while sailing from Liverpool to

Sunset over Mew Island

Mauritius. Of the crew of 15, 7 lost their lives.

In 1882, a new light designed by William Douglass was begun on Mew Island (navigational location 54° 41.9' N 5° 30.7' W). Rubble masonry from the island along with Newry granite decorations were used to build the tower and accommodation. The tower is 121 feet (37 m) tall. The island had its own gas-making plant until 1928; it was the last gas works converted to oil. The lighthouse's current night character is 4 white flashes every 30 seconds. The light with its 5,000,000 candlepower has a nominal range of 24 nautical miles. Mew Island's day mark is a black tower with a white band. On 29 March 1996, the light was automated and the keepers removed. This meant that the golf course they had built for entertainment was allowed to go to weeds.

Mew Island, owned by the CIL, has a number of small associated islands on its south side. This island used to have a thriving fishing and farming community but is now the haven of many species of seabirds and also Grey Seals, which bask on the low reefs.

On the nearby Ards Peninsula, you can find another lighthouse at Donaghadee (navigational location 54° 38.7' N 5° 31.8' W). Located at the end of the harbour wall, it was

Donaghadee harbour with Copeland Islands visible beyond

built in 1836. On 12 May 1900, the lantern and optic were seriously damaged in a fire but were eventually repaired. This was the first light on the Irish coast to be converted to electricity on 2 October 1934. A foghorn was added to the lantern balcony in 1953, which still operates today with 3 blasts every 12 seconds. The white tower is 53 feet (16 m) tall with a nominal range of 18 nautical miles in white and 14 nautical miles in red. Its character is isolating white and red every 4 seconds.

You can see the Donaghadee lighthouse and also catch a boat for day-trips to the 15-minute ferry crossing to the Copeland Islands at Donaghadee Harbour.

Haulbowline

Carlingford Lough lies on Ireland's northeast coast between the Mourne Mountains and the Cooley Peninsula, a narrow strip of Irish Sea between County Down in Northern Ireland and County Louth in the Republic of Ireland. The lough is about 17 miles (27 km) long and 2 miles (3 km) wide at its entrance. Surrounding the lough is an area of natural beauty with low hills, high mountains, woodlands, and little towns and villages each with a wealth of local history and legend. The Vikings named Carlingford Lough - literally "the fjord of Carlinn". There is no record of who Carlinn was or evidence of a permanent Viking settlement here. Until the early twelfth century, the area was divided between a number of ancient Irish kingdoms. These became absorbed into the O'Carroll Kingdom, which had its capital at Louth village, 6 miles (10 km) west of Dundalk. The Anglo-Normans established a permanent settlement here after about 1189 when Bertram de Verdon was granted ownership of the entire Cooley Peninsula. The lough has seen much smuggling of weapons and men into

Haulbowline Northern Ireland. In 1971, the Royal Navy stationed ships in Carlingford Lough to prevent the Irish Republican Army (IRA) from smuggling. In retaliation, the IRA attacked patrol vessels during the 1970s.

In 1817, the merchants of Newry petitioned the Ballast Board of Dublin to replace an old light at Canfield Point with a new light for the lough. George Halpin Senior designed and built a lighthouse on a rock, which is only exposed at low tide. The light was established on 1 September 1824 with a fixed white light (navigational location 54° 1.2' N 6° 4.7' W). A 112-foot (34 m) cut-stone tower stands 105 feet (32 m) above the high-water mark. It was originally painted white but reverted to its natural colour in 1946. The first light was a fixed white beacon with another light on the seaward side to mark the mid-point of the tower. A large ball was hoisted above the lantern to indicate the tide level. The fog bell was struck every 30 seconds. As with many other stations in this book, an explosive device and then an electric horn replaced the bell. Today, the foghorn blows every 30 seconds.

The light beacon on Haulbowline also went through many changes. It went from the original fixed light to occulting and then to flashing. The current character is 3 white flashes every 10 seconds. The light has a nominal range of 17 nautical miles. A rotating red auxiliary light was added to mark entry into the Carlingford Lough Channel with a nominal range of 9 nautical miles. In 1965, Haulbowline became the first major Irish offshore lighthouse to be made completely automatic and controlled from the shore.

One of the worst disasters in Irish maritime history happened within sight of the lighthouse on 3 November 1916 when the *SS Connemara* collided with the Newry-registered ship *Retriever*. The *Connemara* had departed from Greenore with 51 passengers, 31 crew and 4 railway company employees on board in addition to general cargo and livestock. Conditions were clear but a south-southwesterly gale was in progress. Late at night in the channel through Carlingford Bar, the *Retriever* struck the *Connemara* en route from Garston, near Liverpool, bound for Newry with a cargo of coal. Both ships sank immediately with only one survivor, James Boyle, a member of the *Retriever's* crew. It was felt that the cause of the collision was the reduced navigational lights because of the war. The disaster is commemorated a few miles away on a plaque erected in 1996 at the entrance to the Newry Ship Canal.

In order to accommodate larger ships, the channel up the lough and through the bar was deepened in 1868. The Carlingford Lough Commission asked for two leading lights to be built to mark the channel. The lights are screwpile towers with a light on top. The front light on Vidal Bank is 28 feet (9 m) tall (navigational location 54° 1.8' N 6° 5.4' W). At a distance of about 500 yards (462 m) is the second light, Green Island, which has a tower of 45 feet (14 m) (navigational location 54° 2' N 6° 5.7' W). They were established on 28 February 1873 with fixed white lights. In 1922, their character was altered from fixed to occulting and the power source was changed from oil to acetylene. Currently, the Green Island day mark is a 50-foot (15 m) structure with a red triangle pointing down and a white lantern on a screwpile with a character of occulting white every 3 seconds. The Vidal Bank day mark is a 30-foot (9 m) high structure with a red triangle pointing up and a white lantern on a screwpile with a character of occulting white every 2 seconds. Both lights have a nominal range of 11 nautical miles.

Access to Haulbowline is by boat or helicopter. You can check for boats at either Carlingford or Newry. You can see the leading lights at Carlingford, which is found on the R173 south of Newry near Greencastle in County Down.

IRISH LIGHTHOUSES LISTED BY DATE OF ESTABLISHMENT

470 (estimate) - Hook Point
1190 - Youghal
1665 - Charlesfort
1670 - Loop Head
1671 - Baily
1683 - Old Head of Kinsale
1711 - Mew Island
1804 - Aranmore
1806 - Clare Island
1810 - Wicklow Head LV
1811 - Kish Bank LV
1812 - Inishtrahull
1815 - Tuskar
1816 - Blackrock Sligo
1816 - Fanad Head
1817 - Roche's Point
1818 - Wicklow Head
1821 - Metal Man
1824 - Haulbowline
1824 - Kilcredaune
1825 - Dunmore East
1826 - Skelligs
1827 - Inishgort
1829 - Maidens
1830 - Broadhaven
1832 - Tory Island
1835 - Eagle Island
1836 - Donaghadee
1836 - Slyne Head
1837 - Inishowen
1838 - Rotten Island
1839 - Ferris Point
1841 - Cromwell Point
1842 - Drogheda Leading Lights
1843 - Crookhaven

1844 - St John's Point
1847 - Dún Laoghaire East
1847 - Roancarrig
1850 - Ardnakinna
1850 - Dún Laoghaire West
1851 - Ballycotton
1851 - Mine Head
1854 - Angus Rock
1854 - Fastnet
1854 - Little Samphire Island
1854 - Loop Head (new light)
1855 - Dundalk Pile
1856 - Rathlin O'Birne
1856 - Rathlin Island East
1857 - Eeragh
1857 - Inisheer
1858 - Ballinacourty
1860 - Rockabill
1864 - Blackrock Mayo
1864 - Cooper Point
1865 - Kish Bank
1866 - Blacksod Pier
1870 - Inishtearaght
1872 - Scattery Island
1873 - Carlingford Leading Lights
1875 - Ballagh Rocks
1876 - Buncrana Pier
1876 - Dunree
1878 - Galley Head
1878 - Straw Island
1880 - Muglins
1884 - Mew Island
1888 - Chaine Tower
1889 - Bull Rock
1891 - Valentia Leading Lights
1893 - Oyster Island
1902 - Black Head

Oyster Island

GLOSSARY OF TERMS

Acetylene - A fuel used in lighthouses after the 1920s. It was the first fuel to eliminate the need for a keeper to carry oil up the tower, since it could be stored on the ground.

Apparatus - A term used in lighthouse work that denotes the whole optical system housed in the lantern.

Argand lamp - An oil lamp with a circular wick or with several such wicks arranged concentrically.

Argand reflector - A variety of light used in lighthouses that featured a hollow wick in a glass chimney with a silvered parabolic reflector behind to intensify the light. The Argand reflector lamp was named after Aimé Argand, the Swiss inventor who developed the design.

Blue Flag beaches - Beaches that are deemed free from pollution by the EU.

Breakwater - A pier built across the mouth of a harbour to further slow the sea's movement towards the harbour.

Catadioptric - Uses both methods of magnification (catoptric and dioptric). A prism can both reflect and refract, depending upon the angle at which the light falls upon the surface of the glass, whilst a lens usually only refracts. Using a complex combination of prisms and lenses, a very intense and highly magnified beam of light can be created.

Catoptric - The catoptric system involves using a parabolic reflector behind the light, which is often spun around the light to produce the rotating flash one usually associates with lighthouses. The catoptric system is similar to that used in modern flashlights; if you take one apart you will see a parabolic reflector in which the lightbulb is the focal point.

Catwalk - A narrow elevated walkway, allowing the keeper access to light towers built out in the water.

Character of the light - Method of identifying lighthouses at night by their method of flashing, namely the number of flashes per minute and the duration of each.

Day mark - A unique colour, pattern or architecture of towers and other markers used by navigators to establish their location during the day.

Diaphone - A fog signal that consists of a piston driven by compressed air.

Dioptric - Uses a Fresnel lens to concentrate the light. Fresnel lenses take a point light (such as a light bulb) and force the light forward in one direction, as in an overhead projector.

Elevation - The height of a light measured above the Mean High Water of spring tides.

Explosive fog signal - A fog signal in which a keeper electronically detonates explosive charges at regular intervals.

Facets - One of many small pieces of flat mirror glass used to build up parabolic reflectors.

Fixed light - A lighthouse with a steady, non-flashing beam.

Flashing - The light is off longer than it is on.

Focal distance - The distance from the focus to the inner surface of the lens or mirror in an optical system.

Focal plane - The level plane at which the lighthouse's or range light's lens is focused; the height of this plane is measured from mean sea-level.

Fog signal - Any type of audible device that warns mariners from obstacles during periods of heavy fog when the light cannot be seen. Bells, whistles and horns, either manually or power operated, were all used with varying degrees of success.

Fresnel lens - A system of annular prisms that refract and reflect into a beam. Invented in 1821 by Augustin Fresnel, this system captures and focuses up to 70% of the light emitted from the illuminant. Fresnel designed a variety of lens system sizes that he defined by orders. The smallest order of lens is seventh. The sizes of the lenses and their effective range decrease as the order number increases.

Gallery - Outdoor railed walkway encircling the watch room where the keeper monitored the lantern and weather conditions, and cleaned the glass.

GPS - An electronic system for identifying position, GPS is an acronym for Global Positioning System. A GPS receiver decodes each satellite's coded signal to calculate its position.

Hyper-radical - The largest of the order lens but not often used.

Incandescent burner - A burner in which kerosene (paraffin) was heated to form a gas and then burned in a mantle.

Inner range light - The light in a pair of range lights that is situated behind the other as viewed from the water.

Island lighthouse - Lighthouses built on a small island a short distance from the shore.

Isophase light - A light that has equal periods of light and dark.

Lamp - The oil lighting apparatus inside a lens. A lamp was used before electricity powered the illuminant.

Lantern - The portion of the lighthouse structure that houses and protects the lens and illuminant; relative size is described and defined by the size of the lens based on the seven Fresnel orders. Also referred to as the lantern room.

Lantern glass - Glass panes in the lantern that protect the lens and illuminant while allowing the maximum amount of light to pass. Also referred to as "lantern glazing".

Lantern room - A room surrounded by windows, which housed the lighthouse lens.

Leading lights - Two lights some distance apart that when kept inline lead past danger or into a harbour. The term is interchangeable with that of range lights.

Lens - Any glass or transparent material that is shaped to focus light.

Lewis lamp - A variety of light that used a silvered copper reflector behind a glass lens. The design of the Lewis lamp was heavily "borrowed" from that of the Argand reflector, and was named after Winslow Lewis who imported the design from Europe.

Light station - Refers not only to the lighthouse but to all the buildings at the installation supporting the lighthouse, including keepers' quarters, oil house, fog signal building, cisterns, boathouse, workshop, etc. Some light stations have had more than one lighthouse over the years.

Lighthouse tender - Ship used to supply the light and fog signal stations, maintain buoys and service lightships. Today, similar vessels are called buoy tenders.

Lightship - A moored vessel that marked a harbour entrance or a dangerous projection such as a reef where lighthouses could not be constructed. It is also known as a light vessel.

LORAN - An electronic system for identifying position, LORAN is an acronym for Long-Range Radio Navigation. A LORAN receiver measures the differences in the arrival of signals from three or more transmitters to calculate its position.

Murrett - The part of the lantern house between the balcony and the glass usually made of concrete or steel.

Nautical mile - Is equal to 1.15 regular miles.

Nominal range - The distance at which a lighthouse is visible depends on its height when light intensity and other factors are considered equal.

Occulting - The light is usually on for longer periods of time than it is off.

Oil house - A small building, usually made of stone or concrete, which stored oil for light-house lamps. Oil houses were built after paraffin, a highly flammable agent, came into use as an illuminant.

Oil Vapour Lamp - A variety of lamp in which oil is forced into a vaporising chamber, and then into a mantle. It is similar to the Coleman lamps used in camping today.

Optic - A revolving beam of light in a circle at a given rotation speed gives the impression to an observer that the light is flashing, whilst in fact the light is on constantly. It is not the source of the light that rotates, but the apparatus (known as the optic) that creates the beam.

Outer range light - The light in a pair of range lights that is situated in front of the other as viewed from the water.

Parapet - A walkway with railings, which encircled the lamp room.

Pier - A structure extending into navigable waters for use as a landing place, or to protect or form a harbour.

Range - The distance a light can be seen. There are usually two listed. Luminous is the greatest distance the light can be seen by the eye under given atmospheric conditions. Geographic is the distance that the light can be seen until it is blocked from view by the curvature of the earth.

Range lights - A pair of lights placed in such a manner that when they are visually lined up one behind the other, they lead a vessel into harbour. Another name for leading lights.

Refraction - This is when the ray of light passes through a material (such as glass) and is bent as it does so. Fresnel, a Frenchman, discovered the effect in 1822. Prisms of glass when arranged in certain ways can be made to greatly magnify light, again, so long as the light is at the focal point.

Rock lighthouse - A lighthouse built on a small rock in the middle of the sea. Accommodation was limited and the keepers lived in just a few tiny rooms. They slept in a single bedroom in curved bunks known as banana bunks, around the curvature of the tower. Keepers' families lived on the mainland in shore stations. The keepers operated in two teams of three, working one month on duty and one month off duty.

Rotation machine - A motor driven by a falling weight used to revolve many lighthouses' lenses.

Screwpile - 1. A type of piling fitted with a helical fluke that is twisted into the bottom of a body of water. 2. A lighthouse type that employs screwpilings as a primary foundation system.

Shoal - An obstruction found in a shallow area of water such as a sandbar or rock formation.

Shore or land station lighthouse - Lighthouses usually built on headlands and where accommodation was usually large enough to allow the keepers to live with their families.

Shore station - Where the keepers' families from rock or island lights lived.

Siren - A fog signal in which compressed air is forced through slots in a revolving disk.

Ventilation ball - The perforated spherical ball at the apex of the lantern roof that originally provided ventilation for the oil-fired illuminant.

Watch room - A room, usually located immediately beneath the lantern room, outfitted with windows through which a lighthouse keeper could observe water conditions during storm periods.

Wickies - A nickname given to early lighthouse keepers who spent a great deal of their time trimming the wick on the lamp in order to keep it burning brightly, and to minimise sooting.

Metal Man

BIBLIOGRAPHY

Commissioners of Irish Lights, *Lighthouses Currently in Operation*, Commissioners of Irish Lights, February 1999

Collins All Ireland Road Map (9 miles to 1 inch), HarperCollins, 2000
ISBN: 0 00 448967 5

Eagle, John, *An Eagle's View of Irish Lighthouses*, Eagle's Eye Publications, 1999
ISBN: 0 9537271 0 6

Margaret Greenwood et al., *Ireland - The Rough Guide*, The Rough Guides, 1999
ISBN: 1 85828 400 7

Long, Bill, *Bright Light, White Water*, New Island Books, 1997
ISBN: 1 874597 64 2

McCarthy, Kevin, *Lighthouses of Ireland*, Pineapple Press, 1997
ISBN: 1 56164 131 6

McQuillan, Dan, *Ireland Guide*, Open Road Publishing, 1997
ISBN: 1 883323 36 3

Munro, R.W., *Scottish Lighthouses*, Thule Press, 1979
ISBN: 0 906191 32 7

Wilson, T.G., *The Irish Lighthouse Service*, Allen Figgis, 1968

INDEX

T

W

Y

Old Head of Kinsale